# Endorsements

"*How to Become More Successful with Difficult Students* is thought provoking and personifies the plight of young adults is our ever-changing and complex, modern society. His writing stressed the importance of resiliency and perseverance when encountering challenges and learning from those who have "stories" to tell that can change the lives for so many."

    **Gary Mala**—*Former School Superintendent where he was awarded the Presidential Award from the Connecticut Association of Public School Superintendents. College Professor. EASTCONN Executive Director. And he was appointed to U.S. Rep. Elizabeth Esty's (5th District) STEM Advisory Council, and currently chairs the Council's Education Subcommittee.*

"Dan Blanchard's *How to Become More Successful with Difficult Students*, is a must-read for parents, educators, childcare counselors and college students. The contents center not only on classroom management but how to develop a positive rapport with all children & youth, regardless of behavior temperament. The premise of Dan's book stems from his approach to rapport development; emotion drives motion. Relationships are synergized when two or more individuals spend time together, more importantly, they recognize and understand how to navigate each other's emotional intelligence. Dan's utilizes one's emotional intelligence with positive affirmation which results in more cooperation from children. The same tactics are used in adults when leaders require more work productivity from their staff.

    Much of Dan's insight to working with challenging students result in professional coaches who manage complex emotions from professional athletes, as well psychological advantages adults can deploy to children/youth without resulting into power struggles. A highlight from Dan's book is deviating from labeling children with emotional disturbance to treating all children/youth with integrity, value and establishing self-regulation skill sets.

    As a current educator who works in special education, Dan's book applies well with our behavioral management principles & protocols, as a graduate student it only provides more academic substance as well an excellent source of material for primary sources. The literature contents are easy to read; it does not overwhelm readers with over sophisticated educational jargon nor do readers required prior knowledge of classroom behavior issues and educational politics. His book encompasses the history of educational behavioral management as well how educators transition from small, isolated regions into large municipalities where professional development, professional collaboration were required for behavioral management which directly correlates to student success.

It is without hesitation I Daniel Flores, Vice-President of the New Britain Federation of Paraeducators endorse Dan's Blanchard book *How to Become More Successful with Difficult Students* with the highest regards. I encourage all readers to get a copy, apply the techniques Dan outline and implement them in your work environments and family's domiciles."

*Dan Flores—President of New Britain Paraeducators, and workshop presenter/ speaker.*

"Dan Blanchard offers every educator a remarkable book with a practical array of approaches in working with our most challenging students. He turns frustration into success with his wonderful touch of humor, relatable examples, expert wisdom, and genuine belief in every individual... a real gem for everyone working with our youth."

*Connie Bombaci—Retired Teacher and Associate Principal, Author, Speaker, and TV Guest.*

"Dan Blanchard's *How to Become More Successful with Difficult Students; An Educator's Guide to Excellence and Enjoyment in Education*, should be the new teacher's handbook. Dan's guide is a game changing approach for educators to truly understand the many factors faced daily and the importance of keeping order in the class while having fun teaching with a smile."

*Shellye Davis—Hartford President of Paraeducators and member of the National Policy and Planning Committee of the PSRP*

"I have found Dan's new book, *How to Become More Successful with Difficult Students* very helpful as a first year teacher."

*Thomas Cassello—first year teacher*

"I have been working successfully with difficult students for many years as a paraprofessional in a private setting. I thought I knew all the tricks to help these challenging students. However, after becoming a teacher, meeting Dan and reading his book, *How to Become More Successful with Difficult Students*, I learned even more, and now I'm even better at my job now."

*John Lennon—first year teacher*

# How to Become More Successful with DIFFICULT STUDENTS

Daniel Blanchard

Husky Trail Press LLC

Copyright © 2019 by Daniel Blanchard

ISBN 978-1-935258-57-5

Library of Congress Cataloging in Publication Data

www.GranddaddysSecrets.com

Connie Bombaci, Editor

Husky Trail Press LLC
7 Hurlbutt Road, Unit J
Gales Ferry, CT 06335
www.HuskyTrailPress.com
info@huskytrailpress.com

Manufactured in the United States of America

10 9 8 7 6 5 4 3 2 1

# Dedication

*"Without teachers, we are only one generation away
from being launched back into the Dark Ages"*

This book is dedicated to all the committed educators out there who truly are society's unsung heroes as the beacon of light for all of our future generations.

Next to parenting, teaching is by far the most important job in the world in regards to the next generation and the future of our own human race. With teachers, there are real possibilities and bright futures for all of us, even our most challenging students!

# Acknowledgments

It has been a wonderful journey developing this book: *How to Become More Successful with Difficult Students.* I thank all those who have contributed to its creation, either directly or indirectly, as well as all my colleagues and students who have had a hand in making me a better educator. All of my colleagues and students have played a part in making this book possible.

I fully acknowledge my editor, Connie Bombaci, who spent countless hours with me getting what I was trying to say just right. As a former school administrator, Connie Bombaci's professional experience was invaluable to me.

Further thanks need to go to my publisher, Richard LaPorta, of Husky Trail Press. Richard LaPorta has a wealth of knowledge that has helped me put together a better product and a more pleasurable reading experience for our readers.

Finally, I would like to acknowledge my wife, Jennifer, and our five young children. Many late nights, early morning, weekends, as well as vacations were spent with me sitting in our kitchen working on this book. My family waited like saints for me to finish my daily quota of work before we were able to go off and play together. Thanks. I love you all and am truly blessed.

# Contents

# Tough Times for Teachers

Tough times are nothing new for teachers and have always existed in the teaching profession for educators here in the United States. Teaching has never been easy. Obstacles both inside and outside the classroom and in and out of the school building have made things difficult for teachers.

Difficulties infiltrated public education right from the start with the Massachusetts School Law of 1647. This decision stated that a town which grows to the point of more than 50 families must hire a teacher. How do you think they paid for that teacher? The parents had to pay additional taxes and fees to hire that teacher. Eventually, other towns, cities, and states followed Massachusetts' lead on public education. I have to tell you, not everyone agreed with this law, and I'm sure you can imagine that many didn't like paying the additional taxes and fees to hire teachers.

Teaching began as a man's profession. However, during colonial times, Horace Mann eventually convinced the public that it was okay for women to take over the schoolroom. Many didn't like this and didn't think women were qualified. However, the selling point was that women could be paid only a third of what men had received.

One could imagine how this short-sighted selling point could create some complex problems in the teaching profession down the road when it comes to paying equity. Today, the teaching profession is now dominated by women, and they're still fighting for better pay.

In addition, during the colonial times, many worried that the young women, some only 15 years old, would have trouble controlling the unruly children. They were especially concerned about the farm boys who would show up periodically and were taller and older than their young female teachers. Sometimes these big farm boys would discount the teacher and her role of authority and either flirt with her, tease her, or outright defy their smaller and younger female teachers. Furthermore, many worried whether these 15-year-old girls had the education and intellectual abilities needed to be teachers.

But, the communities soon learned that many of these young women did have the intellectual ability needed to be teachers. They also learned that these tiny young women could control, or at least manage the big farm boys. However, with as many as 60 students in one rural schoolhouse, these young female teachers certainly had their work cut out for them.

Today, teachers are still fighting for better class sizes and better student-to-teacher ratios, as well as lower student loads. It's not uncommon for inner city teachers to have five classes of thirty kids or more in each class, as well as, a homeroom and an advisory group. Their student load could easily be anywhere from working with 150-200 students on a daily basis. Additionally, if they coach a sport or run an after-school club, that teacher could add another 30-50 students on a regular basis. That's a lot of kids to see and be responsible for every day.

Around the turn of the 20th Century, immigrants flooded into the United States. Teachers were not only expected to teach the three R's but also to Americanize the immigrants into our American way of life. Teachers were even ordered to wash out the immigrants' mouths with soap when these students reverted to speaking their own language. Wouldn't you agree that those couldn't have been easy days for our teachers?

Oh, and by the way, let's not forget all the Native Americans that our teachers were expected to assimilate into our American culture as well. Teachers were expected to perform the humiliating task of cutting Native American children's hair in a cruel ordered attempt to help these Natives assimilate faster.

Assimilation and Americanization were tough tasks for the young teachers around the turn of the century, to say the least. Today, classrooms are no less diversified and no less challenging than they were a century ago. The names and faces may be different, but that remains a constant and never stops for classroom teachers, especially inner-city school teachers.

Also, around the turn of the 20th Century, teachers were being scrutinized more and more as they found themselves rigidly controlled by the administration, especially in the big cities. Like the factory workers, teachers found themselves victims of Taylorism and the Scientific Management Theory where the common worker frequently wondered why managers were created, and why these managers didn't actually do or even know how to do the work that they were telling others to do.

During this time, teachers' autonomy drastically declined, and teachers resented feeling like the most insignificant cog in the enormous educational and political machine. Teachers felt their work and craft were being devalued, while they were dictated to and spied upon in their efforts. On top of all of that, teachers were paid poorly and had no benefits either.

Teachers eventually realized that they needed to do something. They went through brutal battles to join the up-and-coming unions in order to have a halfway decent chance of a bearable work environment.

Today, teachers are facing many of the same challenges with big business trying to privatize education while painting teachers in a bad light as a way to get what the corporations want, which is the public's tax dollars in the form of educational funding. Sadly, the educational and political machines continue to grind up teachers, weaken unions, and roll over all people who get in their way.

The period from 1930 to 1960 was somewhat calmer. However, that would all eventually change in the educational world once the 1954 Supreme Court Case of Brown v. Board of Education of Topeka, Kansas was handed down. The case ended segregated schools and started all sorts of riots.

Shortly after this, the Vietnam War brought us even more riots and upheavals in the 1960s and 1970s. The disruption continued in the 1983 report, "A Nation at Risk" which was the result of the Soviets launching

Sputnik, the first satellite into orbit in 1957. The report said that our American teachers were underqualified and underpaid, worked in poor conditions, and achieved poor results with our students. Many people are still saying that same thing today, even after countless school reform efforts that have our heads spinning into the outer orbit and our coffers emptying.

Now, we're into the 21st Century, assessing students work, using standardized tests, and basing teacher evaluations on new standards and measurements that have become increasingly controversial. We're also facing a new political climate that is weakening teacher unions to the lowest they've ever been at around or even under 10 %, chipping away at working conditions once again.

Furthermore, the machines are demanding more and more accountability from teachers while at least partially ignoring student accountability, poor student behavior, poor student effort, students' sense of entitlement, and the overall lack of resources for teachers to do their jobs.

With all these obstacles in the way of good teaching and learning, as well as new ones being thrown at educators every single day, one can easily see how teachers have their work cut out for them. But, regardless, these unsung heroes in the teaching ranks carry on against all the odds as the true professionals that they are.

The goal of this book is to help educators become more successful with increasing numbers of difficult students while also creating some excellence and enjoyment in the field of education. I know it's a big order, but I believe it can be done. Let's get started. Let happy days begin again.

# PART 1

## UNDERSTANDING TODAY'S YOUTH

*Chapter One*

# Describing Today's Youth

## I Am The Teacher!

Like many of you out there, I've been teaching students for a long time and grew up during a very different time than today's students. I've been both a special education teacher, as well as a mainstream regular education classroom teacher at the high school level, the middle school level, and the elementary school level. I have taught in public schools, private schools, quasi-private/public schools, international college preparatory schools, and Catholic schools. I have even taught adult education late into the night when my school-age students have gone home for the day. In addition, I have coached multiple sports for many years.

I've seen a lot of different things in the world of education during all of these years of teaching. I've also seen a lot of different students that could be difficult sometimes. I think most of you would agree with me when I say that our students are getting tougher and more difficult to teach each year. Teachers, am I correct, or what? I mean, doesn't it seem like the kids are becoming more and more difficult each and every school year? Yeah… Well, I hear you, and I agree with you. You're right. Today's kids are different and challenging. It's a lot tougher to teach them than it used to be.

## They Are The Students!

When you think about today's kids, or when you hear people talking about today's kids, what are some of the things that people are saying about them? Come on… You know what I'm talking about regarding our kids. Don't be shy. You already know the answer. Who are today's kids? What's the first thing that comes to mind?

Okay, I realize that you don't want to say anything negative about your students. Let's take the easy way out, and let's blame it on someone else. Considering these opinions is how we're going to take a good hard look at our kids. What kind of conversations comes up at family picnics when somebody else mentions today's kids? What are other people saying about today's kids?

Ah… Now you're coming to life. I can already hear some of you saying, "Well, I hear other people say that today's kids have no respect!"

Okay. Good. Now, give me a few more of what other people are saying. What else comes to mind when you think about today's youth?

Yes. You're right again. "No fear." That's true. That's a good one.

You know, I remember when I was a boy, I was always afraid of my dad, the teachers, and my coaches. You're right about that one. I hear you when you say, "No fear," or even "No respect." Today's kids definitely seem different in that category, don't they?

What else? Yup. You're right again when you say, "A lot of anger."

Do you have anything else?

"Instant gratification," you say.

I knew somebody would say that. I knew the instant gratification one was going to pop up somehow. The instant gratification, the microwave society, the impulse thing, or the lack of impulse control—all that stuff that you're spitting out right now about today's youth and their inability to delay gratification—is correct.

Does anybody else have anything to say? Yup. You're right again. "Instigators."

What else can you add?

"Entitled," you say.

I was waiting for somebody to say the entitlement thing. Hey, we're really rolling now. These forbidden buried thoughts are coming to the surface, huh? What other things have you been told or have you overheard? What other things have other people said about today's youth? "They are lazier," right? What? "They are instigators. They are trouble-makers, and they want everything handed to them… right now."

When we think of today's youth, it's like "Oh my gosh, today's kids!"… "This is our future"…"This is what we have to look forward to"… "These are the ones that are going to lead the world and take care of us someday"… Let me say that again in a different way. "These kids are the ones that are going to run this place and determine what happens to us someday?"

Are you scared yet? Well, try not to be. There's still some hope. Teachers, believe it or not, there really is still some enjoyment and excellence in education. We have to know where to look. I'm going to share some information in this fun-to-read, laugh-out-loud-book on how to become more successful with difficult students. How to find that excellence and enjoyment in education, okay?

Teachers, paras, administrators, and all educators simply take a breath and relax. Everything is going to be okay. Students, if any of you are looking at this, there is absolutely nothing to see here. Do you hear me? Absolutely nothing to see here. Just keep moving on, please. Keep going… going… going…this book is adult stuff, not for you…

*Chapter Two*

# Did They Say Those Things About Us

When you think about today's kids, or when you hear people talking about today's kids, what are some of the things that people are saying about them? Come on… You know what I'm talking about regarding our kids. Don't be shy. You already know the answer. Who are today's kids? What's the first thing that comes to mind?

Okay, I realize that you don't want to say anything negative about your students. Let's take the easy way out, and let's blame it on someone else. Considering these opinions is how we're going to a good hard look at our kids. What kind of conversations comes up at family picnics when somebody else mentions today's kids? What are other people saying about today's kids?

Ah…Now you're coming to life. I can already hear some of you saying, "Well, I hear other people say that today's kids have no respect!"

Okay. Good. Now, give me a few more of what other people are saying. What else comes to mind when you think about today's youth?

Yes. You're right again. "No fear." That's true. That's a good one.

You know, I remember when I was a boy, I was always afraid of my dad, the teachers, and my coaches. You're right about that one. I hear you when you say, "No fear," or even "No respect." Today's kids definitely seem different in that category, don't they?

What else? Yup. You're right again when you say, "A lot of anger."

Do you have anything else?

"Instant gratification," you say.

I knew somebody would say that. I knew the instant gratification one was going to pop up somehow. The instant gratification, the microwave society, the impulse thing, or the lack of impulse control—all that stuff that you're spitting out right now about today's youth and their inability to delay gratification—is correct.

Does anybody else have anything to say? Yup. You're right again. "Instigators."

What else can you add?

"Entitled," you say.

I was waiting for somebody to say the entitlement thing. Hey, we're really rolling now. These forbidden buried thoughts are coming to the surface, huh? What other things have you been told or have you overheard? What other things have other people said about today's youth? "They are lazier," right? What? "They are instigators. They are trouble-makers, and they want everything handed to them… right now."

When we think of today's youth, it's like "Oh my gosh, today's kids!"… "This is our future"…"This is what we have to look forward to"… "These are the ones that are going to lead the world and take care of us someday"… Let me say that again in a different way. "These kids are the ones that are going to run this place and determine what happens to us someday?"

Are you scared yet? Well, try not to be. There's still some hope. Teachers, believe it or not, there really is still some enjoyment and excellence in education. We have to know where to look. I'm going to share some information in this fun-to-read, laugh-out-loud-book on how to become more successful with difficult students. How to find that excellence and enjoyment in education, okay?

Teachers, paras, administrators, and all educators simply take a breath and relax. Everything is going to be okay. Students, if any of you are looking at this, there is absolutely nothing to see here. Do you hear me? Absolutely nothing to see here. Just keep moving on, please. Keep going… going… going…this book is adult stuff, not for you…

# PART 2

## SWEET EMOTIONS

*Chapter Three*

# Primitive Emotions

Let me talk to you a little bit about how I've used the secret powers of emotions to create that climate we just talked about in the last chapter. I've had some tough students over the last couple of decades. One of the ways I've created a conducive climate to learning and behaving is by remembering that emotion drives motion in all of us humans, our students included. So, let me say it again, "Emotion" drives motion, okay?

Are you ready for this journey? All right. Good. Now, I'm going to bring us way back to the old primitive, days where primal minds ruled the world. Did you know that many, many years ago we had much smaller skulls? Our human skulls were practically little bumps on the top of our spines. These little bumps were called our first brain or limbic brain. Our first brain or limbic brain essentially consisted of emotions centered on survival, and then eventually, a little bit of spirituality.

Therefore, if we take a hard look at this, the survivalists of yesteryear didn't think much about the dangers approaching them. They didn't just sit there and intellectualize over the perils that were threatening their survival. Rather, their brains just screamed, ***"Run!"*** Whoever ran just a little bit quicker, maybe because they noticed the danger before anyone else, had a chance of living. The saber-tooth tiger was probably going to catch the slower one, the one that saw the threat a little later and eats them instead.

The emotion of fear ruled the day, kept us in motion, and kept us alive.

Have you ever noticed how we still seem to see more bad things today, than good things? Our limbic emotional brain is still there calling the shots from time to time. It demonstrates its powers when our heart starts beating faster, our palms begin getting sweaty, and we aren't thinking straight.

That small primitive bump on the top of our spinal cord is where we and our primitive minds originated. I know. I know. Some of you are already saying that the primitive mind thing is still alive, and, well in your students too, huh? My response to you is… You're right.

The primitive mind is alive and well within our students. Because this is so true, and I'm saying this with the best of intentions, I want to iterate now that the primitive spot in our students' minds is the bullseye that we're aiming for as teachers. That limbic spot is where we are going to meet our students when we're trying to teach them how to stop being so difficult. The rougher our students are, the closer they are to this spot where we can guide them through their emotions.

Now, we all know that over time, all of us, our students too, have developed bigger skulls with bigger brains that contain this newer grey matter that has evolved into our neo-cortex. This newer brain, or our second brain, is called the thinking brain. It grew right over our first brain causing our skulls to become bigger. That's the stage as a species our human development is currently. Well, at least some of us are, right? No. I'm just kidding. We're all there, right? Come on… Say, "Right."

Seriously, here's the amusing thing. We all like to believe that we are in complete control of our lives because we now have these second editions, updated versions, and improved brains that contain a newer and more sophisticated neocortex.

We want to believe that we're modern, rational, and non-emotional creatures, or at least creatures that keep our emotions in check. We want to believe that we're the ones in complete control of ourselves and that our first primitive, emotional brains don't control us anymore, right? Especially us as adults, right? But, believe it or not, in some ways, our first brain still somewhat controls us, especially when we're stressed. As many of us already know, this sometimes irrational and emotional brain definitely controls our children.

You see, the brain scientists to some degree screwed us up. They didn't screw us up on purpose, but, regardless, they did screw us up at least a little bit. What these brain scientists, also known as neuroscientists, did was drop the ball on the stages of maturity regarding our young children's and young students' minds. These brain scientists spent a decade telling us that by the age of ten children have enough brain development to handle advanced learning.

We wonder what the heck is wrong with our kids when they are faced with tasks in which they have to really think, hold their emotions in check, and not act bizarre or out of control. Do you want to know why we wonder what the heck is wrong with them? Well, it's because the brain scientists didn't know what they know now. We all believed these neuroscientists when they told us that our kids could handle the advanced thinking and self-control that took us adults so many years to develop.

The neuroscientists have now discovered that the pre-frontal cortex (PFC), which is right behind our foreheads, actually has a second wave of development during adolescence. That's well after the age ten by the way. That second wave takes place when these kids are trying to learn things like executive functions. You know… that critical thinking stuff, that impulse control stuff, planning their goals stuff, and all that stuff that helps them eventually become responsible and successful adults. Like we are, right?

But, unfortunately, with our youth living outside of the laboratory, something funny happened on the way to the forum… During their teen years, they're still doing crazy stuff, and we're looking at them all weird and wondering what's wrong with them. Why did they do that? Why are they acting like that? Well, the answer is… It's because they haven't fully developed their PFCs yet. Additionally, they won't fully develop them until their early twenties, maybe even their mid-twenties. This revelation may be bad news for some of us adults.

Okay. Back to the kids now. Sadly, some of our youth may never fully develop their PFCs. Some may actually miss out on their developmental stage. Maybe they didn't get the right training, the right situations, or the right critical thinking activities. Maybe they didn't have the right people in their lives to encourage them and challenge them and get them to think critically. Maybe they didn't have the right influences in their lives to help them develop and set their goals and use delayed gratification as a developmental and success strategy.

Unfortunately, since many of our students don't have the perfect conditions in their lives to do these sort of things for them or at least with them, then it becomes our jobs. As their teachers, we help them with their executive functioning development. Like it or not, in today's times, it's now becoming part of our job as a Twenty-First Century Educator.

Times certainly have changed. Parents are very busy and are there a little bit less these days than they used to be. Churches are there a little bit less these days as well. Even the government agencies and do-good charities are there a little bit less. Our students' emotional development is falling on us educators, isn't it? We have to do these extra things to get our students to mature into that next level and help them fully develop their PFCs.

Otherwise, our students will be all over the place acting crazy as usual. Their amygdala, stationed deep within their primitive brain centers, rules the day. Thus, they can't seem to stop and actually think through their behavior before they act. Instead, they merely react like primitive people of yesterday. They can't help but act primitive… as if their minds are still primitive because… well… their minds are still primitive in many ways! After all, everyone knows that we humans do fall in the animal section of the scientific world's classification system.

Hear this again. Earlier, I told you that emotion creates motion. Hence, when we are teaching our students, we need to have patience with them. We need to develop the right kind of climate. We need to meet them where they are in the different spheres of their lives, including the emotional sphere. Where is that special meeting place? It's in the emotional centers of their brains more than the intellectual centers.

As adults, who have a little more self-control and ability to think things through, we need to keep some things in mind. We do need to meet our youth where they presently are in order to be the most effective teachers that we can be.

Hey, **you!** Wake up! Did I just catch you by surprise? Okay. Good. Now, let me ask you this! Have you ever seen a kid put his head down on his desk? Guess what? Few of our students go to bed when they should. They are all tired. But, here's the good news... If we can tap into that thing called emotions that I've been talking about, we can get some more energy and some life out of them. That's a good thing.

They'll pick up their heads off their desks and do some work, and, hopefully at the same time, stop being so damn difficult once we tap into their emotional energy. Let's tap into their emotional side when we're trying to meet them where they are in their PFCs development. If we do this, I believe we'll have a good chance of becoming more successful with our difficult students and helping them to be less troublesome.

*Chapter Four*

# Emotions in Selling

Selling? Emotions? Now I'm really confusing you, huh? You're probably wondering what the heck do emotions in selling have to do with being a great school teacher and in becoming more successful with difficult students, huh? Well, the answer is everything! If we stop and think about it with our newer second neocortex-driven brains, all great salespeople use emotions and a little bit of psychology to get people to do what they want them to do. Remember what I said earlier about emotion creating motion?

Don't be too quick to judge used car salespeople. Perhaps you've used the emotions of selling in your teaching job or even with your own kids at home and don't realize it. Maybe some of you have used selling skills in getting something you want and do know it. Come on... if you pause long enough to reflect and philosophize on this matter, a few of you probably do know a little bit when it comes to using sales techniques.

Hmm... let's think about this for a moment... Let's think about how effective this outside-the-box thinking can be...especially in education. If salespeople can get us grown adults to do things that we may not want to do, like buy a new car, through tapping into our emotions with a little psychology and emotion, then perhaps we can use some of those same magical techniques on our younger and less sophisticated students...

You see, before I go forward with anything else, let me just say this: if as an educator, you're reading only educational books, you're missing out on something special. We educators in this new complex twenty-first century can no longer afford to have such a myopic view of the world in which we live and the world in which we teach. Students are difficult these days, and we need a new bag of tricks because the redundant traditional ones of, "I'm giving you a detention," or calling their homes, doesn't work as effectively any longer.

We educators need to read some psychology books right alongside those educational books. We educators also need to read sales books right alongside our educational books. We need to read all sorts of books right alongside all those educational books. Then, we need to take whatever we can from our wide range of reading to help us get our students to do what's good for them.

I'm not talking about manipulation here. I am talking about doing things that are good for us and good for them. Believe it or not, sometimes buying that new car really is good for us. Most times a student doing their homework is good for them… We can't be too proud to borrow or even steal from other professions and areas of expertise to get our students to do the things that we already know are good for them.

You see, every great salesperson knows that people don't buy by logic. People say they make their buying decisions based on logic, but they don't. People are hesitant to admit that the real reason they bought that car was that it was red. That's right. It was red. Well, it was red, and it was fast too (Emotional Brain- 1st Place). When they are driving the red, fast car home and their emotions are shifting into overdrive, their emotional energy is pumping along with the radio tunes. They are genuinely excited about driving that new red fast car.

However, eventually, they begin thinking about what they're going to tell their family and friends about why they bought this brand new, red fast car. Somehow telling them that the car was red, or even that it was red and fast, doesn't seem like such a good idea anymore. What do they do? They quickly come up with the explanation, "Hey, this car gets good gas mileage, and it was on sale too." That's how they'll rationalize (Thinking Brain- 2nd Place) their decision to their family and friends. They use their thinking brain while trying to mute their emotional 1st brain and trying to keep themselves from looking foolish.

The truth is that even we, adults, act on emotion. If this sales approach isn't sophisticated enough for the academia in you, then let's say the truth is that we, teachers, and our students act on pathos. We just can't seem to outgrow that emotionally attractive stuff or the pathos appeal fully. It's a fact. We're emotional beings. We can try to say that we don't solely act on our emotions, but, truthfully, many times that is what we're doing. We're lying to ourselves about it when we say that we're not.

All good salespeople know how emotions and pathos drive logic or the logos in us as the academia people out there are screaming out right now. People buy on emotion and back up their decisions with logic. Their first mind, the emotional one, takes the lead. Then, when they are driving home in their new red, fast car, the second mind, the neocortex, kicks into gear. Specifically, the pre-frontal cortex (PFC) in the neocortex, which is located right behind our foreheads, usually gets its turn only after the amygdala, which resides deep in the first emotional brain, does what it's going to do.

After the fact, the PFC finally says, "Okay, how can I explain this emotional behavior in a way that is rational in thinking?" As rational thinking beings with big neocortex brains, we have to come up with a logical way of explaining to our family, our friends, and even ourselves, why we bought this car. We don't want to look like dummies buying this freaking red, fast car.

That's how our adult minds work. Similarly, when our students do something spontaneously, they have to rationalize it too by saying something like, "The teacher doesn't like me." We've all seen this behavior in kids. Life works this way. If we, adults, can be emotionally moved to act, so can our students. As teachers, we have to use our logic and learn how to rev up the emotions in our classes by becoming better salespeople for our products of a good education, good student choices, and good student behavior.

We have to sell our students on the fact that their efforts are going to be worth the reward of doing what we ask them to do so they can get a good education. Every good salesperson knows the key is to get the customer to like them, trust them, and want to do business with them. We educators have to get our students to do the same thing as we're emotionally revving up their engines and getting them to like us, trust us, and want to do business with us. Then, it's on them to figure out how they're going to explain to their friends and family that they like us, like going to our class, and even like doing some of their classwork.

*Chapter Five*

# Emotions in Sports

Hopefully, this chapter won't confuse you as much as I did in the last chapter with all those radical ideas of learning how to be a salesperson. Although, I imagine some of you out there looking at this chapter right now might be wondering what the heck emotions in sports have to do with being an excellent schoolteacher. Okay, give me a minute or two in this chapter, and I'll explain it to you.

With a bit of luck, I was a good, little salesperson in the last chapter and was able to successfully explain to you how powerful the secret weapon of emotions is in education. With any good fortune, I was able to get you to like me, trust me, and want to do business with me. Now, with that said, let's get down to business here in the educational sports' world. After all, this one shouldn't be as big of a leap as the last chapter. I mean, we've all seen sports' programs at our local schools, right? Schools and sports just seem to go together. Well, at least on the surface level, sports and schools seem to go better together than sales and school, right?

Oh, speaking of emotions, you want to know who is really good at emotional button-pushing? Coaches are very good at pushing emotional buttons and getting an emotional rise and better performance out of their players.

Go to any college football, baseball, basketball, wrestling, or whatever sport you can find on the college levels, the professional levels, the international and the Olympic levels, or even the high school levels. We'll see these coaches pushing the emotional buttons of their players. These coaches get peak performances out of their athletes, which usually adds up to a lot of outstanding play, victories, and sometimes even fortune and fame. These coaches keep their jobs by pushing their athletes' emotional buttons and putting wins in the win column.

Believe it or not, sometimes coaches push their athletes' emotional piss-them-off button. Sometimes, it's the make-me-proud-emotional button. Maybe, it's the emotional scare-the-heck-out-of-them button. Regardless of how coaches do it, or which buttons they push, great coaches press their players' emotional buttons all day long, every day of the season, and even days in the off-season.

Remarkable coaches have a long history of creating peak performances in their athletes. It's just a common fact that outstanding coaches get their players to perform. Keep that in mind and imagine if we could get a quarter of that performance out of our students in the classroom. Reaching that feat would consist of us being able to push one-fourth of our students' emotional buttons. Imagine if we could get our students to perform once in a while like coaches repeatedly get their athletes to accomplish? Imagine if we could get our students to invest in themselves just half of what the great coaches and great salespeople get their people to dedicate?

You see, part of the problem is that once we enter the educational world, most people don't think that the sales world or sports world logically fits in that space. Most people in the educational world tend to look at this emotional stuff as if it was too Pollyannaish, was beneath their intellect, or wouldn't work anyway. The scholarly world wants mere facts. Yup. Just the facts.

Guess what? These highly educated people are wrong. Until they look outside of their pretty, little boxes that are flawlessly colored within all the lines, I believe that the sports coaches and salespeople will continue to monopolize the exceedingly effective ways of getting people to move and perform. People in these professions have figured it out. Have the educators figured it out? Are we brave enough to at least try emotional button-pushing in the educational world and then hold our judgment until later—until after we've seen some of the results?

Hey, if you really think about it, why can't we, teachers, figure out and use this emotional button-pushing thing, too? Why can't we get better performances out of our students like the performances coaches get out of their athletes? Why can't we sell our educational product to the proud, new owner of a better, grade-point average (GPA) like salespeople sell us that new, red, fast car?

If we're not getting what we want out of our students, some of it has to do with the fact that we are not pushing their emotional buttons enough. Remember, emotion creates motion. It's a real phenomenon. It does work. If we want our kids to get their heads up off of their desks, get up, get moving, do their assignments, and stop being dreadfully difficult, then we're going to have to figure out how to push some of those emotional buttons in our students. Maybe we need to take a short walk down to the football coach's office and find out how he or she does it. We need to learn how to hit those buttons while combining all the other stuff that will make them winners.

I say, "Let's do this! Let's win again and be proud of our performance and our students' performance in The World of Education!"

# PART 3

## WHAT DO WE WANT?

*Chapter Six*

# What Do We All Want?

What is it that we all want besides the basics of air, water, food, and shelter? Does anybody have any suggestions? What is it that we all honestly want?

"A good life," you say. Perfect. I'm glad you mentioned that because you're right. We all do want a good life. What else do we all want?

"We want to be respected," you say. Yeah. You're right again. We all do want to be respected. Therefore, what I hear so far from you is that we all want to have a good life, and we want to be respected, right?

What else do you think we, teachers, want?

Yeah… You're right again. We want to be excited about our jobs. Furthermore, we want to be excited about our life, in addition to being appreciated, huh? You see, these are some of the things that we all want. I believe that you would agree with me when I say that if we want these things, then perhaps our students might want some of these things as well, right?

It's probably not too far of a stretch to say that our students probably want to feel appreciated. Believe it or not, they probably also want to feel excited about going to school—like we want to feel excited about going to work every day, correct? Believe it or not, I bet our students want to feel excited about spending time with their teachers. Psss… that's us—the educators.

Trust me. Our students really do want to feel excited about the time they spend with us. They want to be excited about being in our classrooms. They want to feel excited about being on the football field or wrestling mat, the basketball court, or the baseball diamond. They want to be excited about being in math class, gym class, on stage, or wherever they are spending time during their day with us adults...the educators! No, I didn't say "Terminators." I said, "Educators."

Trust me. The idea of our students wanting what we want makes complete sense when we think about human nature and the far less desirable alternative of not enjoying their time in school with us. Our students are little versions of us. Since we would rather be excited than bored, happy over angry, it makes sense that they would want to be excited and happy rather than bored or angry. Hey, if we're going to be spending time in school anyway, then it might as well be a good time, right? I mean, come on now, who wants to choose to have a bad time over a good time? Even our students wouldn't pick a bad time over a good time… Well, at least, I hope they wouldn't…

I ask you once again to trust me. Our students want a lot of the same things that we want. One of those things they want is to be excited about their time in school with us, and we want to be excited about the time we spend with them making this world a better place. Do you want to know what else we all want? We all want to win. Let's go out there and be the best possible educators that we can be, and let's all try to win together. After all, we're all in this together, so we might as well all win together! Hey, it's better than losing, wouldn't you agree? Hey, that's a tie-down! What a great teaching strategy! Oh, you're probably not sure what a tie-down is, huh? Well, keep reading, you'll find out eventually…

*Chapter Seven*

# Climate

The big question is how do we help our students feel excited about spending time with us at school? How are we going to create excitement about education and winning happen again within the educational world? Well, the simple answer is... We're going to start the process of being excited and winning with ourselves and within our classroom through... **Climate!**

We are going to take charge of our own thoughts and the climate that we create in our classrooms on a daily basis. Now, I already know what some of you are saying, "Dan, if you only knew some of the students I had? Little Billy... He'll freaking blow any kind of climate that I try to create right out of the water within the first five minutes of class." Some of you are even saying, "Hey, I come into school every day, and I try to create a good climate. Some days it's impossible to maintain a good climate when the kids clearly won't let me."

Listen, I hear you. I feel your pain. I really do. I know exactly what you're talking about and feeling because I have personally been there and felt the pain that you're referring to here. I, too, as a teacher, have felt the pain more times than I can remember. I know the pain you're talking about all too well. However...

The reality is that Little Billy or little Jose or little Suzy or little Anella... or little whoever... are kids. Literally, they are the kids, and we are the adults. It's not up to the kids to create the climate. No. That would be irresponsible of us to assume that it's up to the kids. The more responsible job of creating the climate goes to the adults. If we don't generate that climate as the adults, then the positive, caring atmosphere that we all need to succeed and be happy will not happen. Period. The kids won't do it… Didn't you ever watch that movie, Lord of the Flies? You know what happens when kids are left to their own devices without any adults around, even if it is living on a beautiful beach and a beautiful island…They stole Piggy's classes, did war dances, and all sorts of other dangerous things in the dark.

No. Don't let them do it. We have to do it! We have to create the climate. We can't permit the immature kids to create the climate, even if they are taller than we are…Could you imagine if we did allow them to create the climate? Hey, here's the deal… I already know that some of us don't have to wonder what this would look like. Some of us have already lived it, right? The pain is fresh in our minds and tightening around our hearts, isn't it? As a matter of fact, sometimes that pain even wakes us up out of our sleep, huh?

You need to realize that most of our students don't know the first thing about how to create a positive and exciting Climate. Creating a good climate is up to us. As the adults, we have to construct that productive and fun climate. Hey, think about it. If we're not going to be positive and have at least a little bit of fun at work, then it stinks to go to work, doesn't it? Yeah. Sure it does. Guess what? It stinks to be a student in that same environment and climate.

Let me ask you something. Have you ever had that Sunday night, heart-pounding thing? Ever get those sweaty palms or those butterflies in your stomach on Sunday night? We've all had this feeling, haven't we? Plus, we all know why it's happening, don't we? It's happening because we know that Monday morning is right around the corner.

What about that end-of-the-summer feeling? Same sort of thing as that Sunday night feeling, isn't it? Butterflies in our stomach, right? Those butterflies disappeared for a little while over the summer, huh? But near the end of the summer, they are back. We can't seem to get those dang butterflies to leave us alone. If they're not going to leave us alone, wouldn't it be nice to get them to fly sort of formation that's not upsetting our stomach and nerves?

I'm sure you'd all agree with me when I say that the last thing we all want is to feel those butterflies messing with us again, right? What? Are some of you saying that your butterflies still haven't left this school year? Okay. All kidding put aside. Wouldn't it be nice if we all enjoyed going to work? Well, for this to happen, we have to take charge of our classroom environment. We have to create that fun and exciting climate. We can't let all the excuses get in the way. I know there are a lot of good reasons out there. Bottom line, they are still just excuses, right? Well, we can't let those excuses stop us anymore from enjoying our jobs and, hopefully, our careers as educators.

Think positive. Hey, of course, little Billy is going to be a pain in the butt. Of course, kids are difficult. However, the kids and the climate can be molded if we straightforwardly take charge and make it happen. The kids aren't going to make it happen. Creating classroom climate isn't going to happen all by itself. Well, the kind of environment that we want to happen won't happen all by itself.

Listen, this is not some hokey pokey, Pollyanna, pseudo-science, or made-up idea. Classroom climate actually does exist! It's true. I'm not lying. Trust me. I wouldn't lie to you about something like this. Guess what? We need to mold that climate more to our liking if we're indeed going to enjoy our students and our school year.

The climate is our responsibility. Now, don't go getting all crazy because I just used that word, "responsibility." Some of you are probably moaning and saying, "Oh great. Another thing we're responsible for..." Hey, responsibility doesn't have to be another four-letter word. I always say to turn your frown upside down, and now I'm going to say to turn that word responsibility backward. You see, responsibility turned backward is nothing more than having the ability to respond. That's what we all want... the ability to respond... like a superhero... The ability to respond to anything thrown at us. Let's go ahead, and let's all take responsibility for our classroom climate!

*Chapter Eight*

# Relationships Are Everything

What else can we do to build a positive and exciting climate that will help create optimal learning within our classrooms while diminishing the behavior disruptions? Well, the answer is quite simple. Not an easy one, but certainly a simple one. Are you ready? Good. Here it is. Someone give me a drum roll. Please... The answer is... Relationships. Relationships are everything! Come on everyone... Repeat after me... "Relationships are everything!"

Consider this for a moment. I remember when I was wrestling and playing football as a youth. During those years of playing sports, I would have done anything for my team as well as my coach. Furthermore, I remember many years later as an adult, when I was coaching wrestling and football. During those years, I had kids in both sports that would have gone through brick walls for me. They would have done anything I asked them to do.

At the same time during those years, I was also teaching school, and I had an extremely tough time getting my students to do some of the most basic things they needed to do in order to succeed. Going through a brick wall definitely was out of the question for these kids. That wasn't even part of the equation in those classrooms where I was trying to teach my students success and academic skills.

However, the funny thing is that I had some of those same students as athletes. Right after school dismissal, somehow, they magically transformed into those kids who gave their all, and even more for me. It wasn't adding up. I often wondered, could these possibly be the same kids who gave me trouble in English class?

This crazy Dr. Jekyll and Mr. Hyde phenomena got me to consider what the heck was going on here. What the heck was causing the difference between the world of education between 7:00 – 3:00 and the world of sports after 3:00?

I wondered, how could these same kids be so different? During the school hour, they were a certain kind of person (No expletives here, please). Then after school, they became completely different people. I thought, what if I could get them to stop acting bipolar and perform consistently? Wouldn't it be nice to get our students to want to go through a brick wall for us during school hours too? But, "How?" I wondered…

I'll tell you how. Educators build strong and lasting relationships with our students. By forming and cementing ties with them, especially the tough ones, we'll see that they will begin to at least think about going through some brick walls for us during those dreaded school hours.

Hey, to tell you the truth, this isn't rocket science. I think we all can admit that we want good, solid relationships. Why wouldn't our students want them too? Besides, we probably already knew this relationship thing is a good thing. We all want relationships, and we all want to go through brick walls for people. It's in our DNA.

In order to prove this, let's go way back again, okay? If we think about our early ancestors, this going through-the-brick-wall thing becomes a lot clearer. Here it is in a nutshell. If I protect you, and you protect me in return, then we're going to have a better chance of survival. It's like some kind of tribal security from our ancient ancestors that still resides in our DNA.

Next, let's take another look at the primitive brain—the emotional brain. You already know this is the first or limbic brain that we talked about earlier. Our emotional centers in our brains signify everything because it means our survival. These emotional centers in our first brain helped us survive when bigger and stronger animals chased us. From way back, survival was based on relationships with other clansmen or tribesmen. Relationships were essential to living and not being some bigger animal's dinner.

Think about what I'm saying in its most basic form. It's in my best interest to make sure you survive. Because the next time there is a threat to me, you owe me one, and we're stronger as a team of two rather than an individual. We're much stronger as a 10, 50, or even 100-person team. On the most basic primal level, it's in our best interest to make sure we have good relationships with all of the people that we spend our time with throughout the day.

That primitive, emotional mindset based on survival is still there inside our modern-day skulls, all wrapped up in that grey matter stuff. Because of that, we naturally build relationships—we build relationships with our students, our athletes, our kids, our peers, and whomever else is in our lives. Building these relationships makes things change for the better. We won't see our comrades wrestle a bear to the ground, or even throw rocks at it from afar, but we may eventually see them go through brick walls for us. Well, I'll tell you the truth. They don't really go through brick walls for us, but you know what I mean, right? They stand by us during good and bad times, right? They'll do just about anything we ask them to do, right? As long as it's legal, right?

With that said, let's begin creating better relationships with our students. Are you ready? Good. Here we go. Believe it or not, the first day of school isn't the best time to jump straight into the curriculum. On day one of every year, I work on relationship building with my students first and foremost. Sometimes on day two, I'm still working on relationship building, and maybe I'm peeking into the curriculum. Day three, I'm glimpsing a little bit more into the curriculum and still working on those relationships. As a matter of fact, even when the curriculum is running full speed, I am still working on those relationships every single day of the school year… We have too!

Some of you teachers out there may not understand what I'm doing. Some may even think that I'm putting myself behind in my department's curriculum pacing guide. Don't you worry one little bit about this, okay? When we focus on relationship builders, it will mean that later in the school year we won't be one of those teachers who is having behavioral problems and is stopping, starting, stopping, starting, and continually stopping to address continuous poor and disruptive behaviors. We're not getting chased down and eaten up by the bigger, stronger, bad-behavior animals.

We're breezing through our curriculum in overdrive because we have fewer poor behaviors while other teachers are running hot and ruining their brakes on their educational vehicle because of all the starting and stopping due to the disruptive behaviors. Guess what? Eventually, we're not behind in our curriculum, at all, are we?

The bottom line is that it's worth the effort and time to start a little slower and more deliberate at the beginning like a tortoise, isn't it? The hare in the next classroom only looks like he's winning in the beginning. But, we all know what happens in the end, don't we? Even when things seem all screwed up, remember to trust the process and always work on those relationships every single day of the school year. It's worth it. It puts us front and center with our students, and it doesn't put us behind our colleagues.

You know, in a way, the whole relationships thing goes back to the psychology of sales that I had mentioned earlier in this book. Huh? Hey, believe it or not, we're all salesmen. We're all trying to sell our students something, whether it's the product of "It's worth it to behave and do your work," or, "Work up to your potential." It's still Sales 101. Think about it. What are we honestly trying to do through building positive relationships with our students? It's the same thing all good salesmen are trying to do when they aim to get their clients to like them, trust them, and want to do business with them.

Let's repeat that. "I want my students to like me, trust me, and want to do business with me." If you can get that from them, you now have something extraordinary. You will have something exceedingly special if you comprehend on a deep level what I'm saying to you here. As teachers, parents, coaches, and adults in general, it makes a lot of sense to work and get our youths to like us, trust us, and want to do business with us—have a good relationship with us.

Hey, listen, it's a fact that building good relationships with our students and athletes can pay big dividends down the road. Not too long ago, I was teaching a freshman social studies class, and I had to repeatedly tell a student that I needed him to open his book so we could get started. Once again, he didn't. He continued to refuse and give me a hard time. At that same moment, one of my former students just happened to be walking down the hallway while this scene was taking place. He could see into the classroom and hear what was going on. I didn't know it at the time, but my former student entered the class and came up right behind me. Now, teachers, let's keep what I'm about to share with you just between us, as we celebrate and wish this sort of thing could happen more often, okay? Shh… Now don't tell anybody, but this is what happened.

My former student walked into my classroom, stood right behind me, gave the kid who was misbehaving an incredibly mean look, and said, "You better open your book and keep your mouth shut, or I'll find you later. And don't you ever disrespect my teacher again!" He was an overpowering upperclassman, and this defiant kid was a pint-sized, immature freshman. End of story. I didn't need to say a thing after that.

When we're building those relationships, a good strategy is to get our kids to help us, especially if they are the tough ones. One of the things I like to do the first few days of school is to take a good look at all of my students and figure out who might be the most primitive or difficult. Those are the ones I want to make my tribesmen first. Those tougher ones are the first ones who I'm going to buddy up with and make my new clansmen. I spend my initial energy on them. The well-behaved, easy ones are just that—easy. Once things are running smoothly, I can spend a lot more time with them.

The compliant students are most likely going to be our buddies anyway. But, if we can engage the tough ones right in the beginning—like us, trust us, and want to do business with us—then we have a greater chance of having a better school year, and so do they. If we can get the tough ones on our side from the start, it makes everything else easier.

However, if we don't do this buddying-up thing with the difficult ones, eventually those tough ones are going to recruit allies or tribesmen of their own to band together against us. But, if we can get the tough ones on our side immediately, they will help us attract the other kids to our team, as well. The other students will merely follow suit because they don't have anyone else to follow. We have to remember—don't butt heads with the tough kids. They have a way of recruiting kids to be part of their rebellion and head-butting competition, and then, our school year gets dreadfully long.

Some of you teachers out there have already had a couple of those long years that I'm talking about—when you have to deal with the tough ones recruiting others, haven't you? Come on… Tell the truth. I certainly know that I have.

Here's how it snowballs on us. The dynamics of every class is that we have some good kids, some kids sitting on the fence, and usually a few rougher kids. If the rough kids start acting up, the ones sitting on the fence will join their camp. Then, either the good ones will stay out of it completely, which is of no help to us, or they will try to fit in with the chaotic environment by adding to the unruliness while we're trying to teach. The situation becomes even worse. It becomes a nightmare. None of us teachers should have to live or work like that. We mustn't live like that. We have to win over the tough ones first because then they will help us keep all the others in line.

Finally, I'm a big believer in thoroughly knowing our subject content. Being the expert is the only way we'll know how to make the material interesting, more enjoyable, and accessible for our students, which means better behavior.

However, don't fall into the trap that some teachers fall into when they have weak relationships with their students. These teachers always complain about their students. They boldly proclaim their absurd proclamations that they teach math, or they teach English. They say phooey on these kids for not paying attention. Well, I believe these teachers have it backward. They teach students math. They teach students English.

While I repeat that we must thoroughly know our content, we must remember that the students always come first! The academic material comes second.

Hang on tight because the rest of this book is going to move fast. I'm going to share with you a whole bunch of other great stuff, great information, and great resources. You'll get a lot of great strategies on how to build those relationships, as well as little tricks that get the kids to like you, trust you, and want to do business with you through working harder for you and cooperating with you more often.

# PART FOUR

## OUR CREATION

*Chapter Nine*

# Setting the Tone Right Away

The process of building relationships, building the ideal climate, and building expectations with us and our need to set the tone begins immediately. First impressions do matter. Therefore, I set the tone by starting on day one with my routine of meeting my students at the door. I don't let them into the classroom until I talk to them, shake their hand, high-five them, or something similar. After I have built that good first impression, I'm ready to send them into the classroom. Hopefully, by then, they think that this guy seems pretty cool. With any luck, they're thinking, "Hey, he met me at the door, talked to me, smiled, laughed, and did all that other good stuff. Maybe he's okay…"

The very next thing I do is tell them where they are going to sit. I say, "Andrey, your seat's right there. Right there. Got it? Right there." Subsequently, Audrey looks around and thinks, "Huh." I catch them off guard by telling them what to do after I was just so pleasant to them upon our first meeting at the door. They're not expecting this authoritative command out of me.

Then Maria comes to my door, and I catch her right before she can get into the classroom. Greeting them is essential on that first day of school. I don't let any of them into the my room before I talk to them, okay? I say something like, "Hey, I'm so glad you're in my class, Maria. Your seat's right there." After a while, a couple of kids will exclaim in surprise, "We've got assigned seats?" I reply, "Yup," with the biggest smile on my face that you could imagine. That big crazy smile confuses them even more than the nice guy telling them what to do. With a confused look on their faces, some of them even mumble, "Why?"

Okay, teachers, there are a couple of things going on here that I need to tell you about right now. One, I want the first impression of me to be the guy that's at the door who is showing that he already cares about his students, even though he just met them. I want to be the guy with high energy. Smiling. The good guy at the door. The good guy that is already organized and has already been working hard. The guy who's their boss. Have you got that? I'm in charge of them. I'm their boss. I need to set that tone from the very first impression. I'm the adult-boss. They are the kid-followers.

They're not going to walk into my room and sit wherever the heck they want and think that they are in charge. They're not going to put their feet up. They're not going to find that back corner and then try to occupy it like they just invaded it, and now own it. I firmly say, "Nope. We're going in alphabetical order." In my nicest commanding, former military voice, I say, "You're there. You're there. You're there. And, you're there." Oh, by the way, I don't actually say, "You're…". I use their names when I'm bossing them around because that's the nice way to boss kids around.

When they complain, which they will, and they whine, "Why are we alphabetical?" I might respond, "Listen, guys, I have so many great things to teach you this year. We're going to be rocking and rolling in this class all year long. The last thing I want to do is slow down for when taking attendance, collecting papers, and handing out papers. I also have to make sure I'm not screwing any of that silly stuff up. When we sit in alphabetical order, all that administrative and non-teaching junk goes faster and easier. I also make fewer mistakes with crediting you for your work. I see quicker who is here and who is not here. I am able to go, 'Boom—that seat is empty, so Maria is absent.' That's it. Quick. Simple. Done. This way I'm not accidentally marking people absent when they are here, and I'm teaching you guys awesome stuff within seconds of the starting bell. I don't want you to miss any of the great things that I have for you this year!"

They are like, "This guy is freaking crazy. Look at his energy. Very high energy. How does a teacher have such high energy? Is he some sort of spaz or something? Maybe he's very different. Maybe he has something good to teach us."

You see, I set the tone right away. Done. Finished. Within the first few minutes of day one, my students already sense that I'm friendly, I'm in charge, and I have a sense of humor and some urgency to me. I might even be a little weird. That's a good thing because we already know kids are a little weird too, so they naturally like weird things. At the very least, they are a little intrigued by whacky things, like me, and maybe someday even you. Hey, we all know how kids love intrigue. Heck, we all love intrigue. I bet none of your college teacher-preparatory classes taught you any of that stuff, huh? Hey, isn't that another tie-down. Hold on to that thought—"tie-down." It is coming later in this book.

Believe it or not, I've even done this seating chart thing in my adult education classes, even though adult education is a little bit different. I've used the same strategies with them to help them immediately understand that I'm the weird friendly guy in charge. This approach can be used in adult education too and is executed a bit differently. Now, I know some of you are not going to be comfortable telling the young adults, and I do mean young these days, "You're there. You're there. And, you're there." You're probably thinking this method is going to sound too confrontational with your mature classes, huh?

Instead, try this little trick that I've performed in adult education classes. When the kids come in, I mean when the young adults come in, I let them sit where they want. Right after they settle in, I go through with my clipboard starting with the last student in the last row. I say something like, "So, what's your name?"

"Robin," she responds.

"So, Robin, this is where you're sitting?" I ask.

She seems to be thinking, "Of course, this where I'm sitting. Can't you see?"

"You're sitting right here, right?"

Her puzzled look conveys, "What is wrong with this guy? He can't see that I'm sitting right here?"

"Okay, Robin. This seat is where you're sitting from now on. "

Then I say to the person right next to Robin, "What's your name?"

You see, I'm making it known that I'm taking attendance, but at the same time, I'm sneaking up on people because I'm coming from the back of the room. Simultaneously, I'm getting a lot of easy buy-in and agreement that this is where they're sitting for the semester.

The girl right next to Robin responds that her name is Kate. I reply, "Kate. This is where you're sitting. You're sitting right here, right now. Right? That's where you're sitting right now? Okay, so you're sitting right here, Kate."

Kate will look at me like I'm totally weird. But, guess what I have? I have the beginning of a seating chart. I do this same strange thing to all my adult education students as they're working on their assignment. My seating chart is complete, and I didn't even appear to be bossing these young adults around. I was only a little unconventional. However, on top of that weirdness, I've already started to show them who was in charge.

Now and then they say, "Why are you doing this?" I just throw them my whole excited act about learning awesome stuff, and I can't slow down for this administration minutia. I tell them, "I want to teach! I don't want to make any dumb mistakes when it comes to giving credit for the work completed or giving credit for attending my class."

I'm telling you, my fellow teachers out there, this crazy stuff works. It really does work. If seating charts work in adult education, guess what? Your high school kids aren't too old for a seating chart either. They aren't too old to be told where to sit or what to do. Get those crazy ideas out of your heads that they're too grown up now, and it's all a lost cause. Take charge of your class right from the start.

Now, you're supportive and fun and full of high energy on one side, and you're leveling it off with you're the boss on the other side. You're telling your students, "Hey, there's a new sheriff in town, but he's a cool, Six-Shooter Sheriff Dude."

Teachers, please remember this: If they are going to be in our classrooms, then they must learn that they are not the boss. They are the kids. Kids cannot be the bosses of the adults. Maybe they get away with that craziness in their homes. But, not here. Not in school. While in school, they are kids. Okay? Moreover, kids don't have any power in school. We, adults, have all the power. Now, repeat after me… We, adults, have all the power in school! Good! Now, you're learning! We are the adults, and this makes us the bosses. They are the kids. Therefore, they are not the bosses.

*Chapter Ten*

# Routines

The next thing I do to help my students normalize their behaviors and feel comfortable in my class is… routines. That's right. Routines. Routines are quite simple to do, but they are equally as simple not to do. Trust me. Routines are powerful. Every school day when my students come to my doorway, the same ritual starts immediately. I offer my hand for them to shake, high five, low five, side five, fist pump, or some fancy handshake right at the classroom door.

Want to know what we do next? I will share that with you in a moment. But first, let me tell you a quick little story. Have you ever watched Notre Dame Football? Have you seen when the Notre Dame Football players run out of locker room onto the field, and they all slap the sign above the entrance to the stadium that says, *"Play Like A Champion"*? This little ritual helps pump Notre Dame up and gets them ready to go out there and kick some butt. The Fighting Irish are psychologically ready after slapping their Creed to Play Like A Champion—to go to any length to succeed.

One day while watching this little Notre Dame ritual on television, I wondered why can't I use this same psychological, motivational tactic in my classroom to try and get my students to perform better? Why can't I make this little ritual part of my class routine?

As a result, every single day when my students come into my classroom, the first thing they do is shake my hand. Next, they look for the *"Play Like*

*A Champion*" sign that I have taped to the outside wall at the entrance of my classroom, and they slap it just like Notre Dame slaps their sign. My students slap it hard, and we all get goosebumps running down our spines when we hear that slapping noise. This little ritual of *"Play Like A Champion"* is part of my Class Creed and routine. I want my students to consistently believe that they are champions and perform like they are champions every day in my classroom.

The simple little act of slapping the *Class Creed* of *"Play Like A Champion"* creates more physical movement and gets my students emotionally charged up and feeling like winners. This little ritual helps them feel as if they can do something worthwhile in my class and as well as in life. The truth is that they can do something worthwhile with their lives because it says it right there in the *Class Creed* in the *"Playing Like A Champion"* poster that they slap every day.

If they can see it, read it, touch it, and talk about it, then they can perceive it, believe it, and achieve it. I'm trying to change my students' thinking and make victors out of them—not helpless victims. They need to stop thinking like victims and start thinking like victors.

Here is what the *Class Creed* looks like on my classroom wall that they slap on the way into class and on the way out:

What's happening in my class with the routines that we share every day? Well, let's take a closer look and find out.

First, my students meet me at the door with a shake, high five, fist pump, or whatever. Second, they slap the *Class Creed* of *"Playing Like A Champion."* Then, they walk into my class feeling pumped. Imagine that! A kid feels pumped coming into our classrooms. Best of all, it wasn't hard to accomplish. Let me repeat that. They are feeling pumped coming into my room, and it wasn't that hard to do.

Do you want to know why it's not that hard to do? It's not that hard to do because it's all part of the routine they participate in every day. Right after they shake my hand, fist pump, and slap the *Class Creed*, they walk

# Class Creed

*Never think like a victim. Don't waste energy casting blame. Focus on the goal and work day by day to overcome the obstacles in your path. Ask for help when you need it, and help others when you can. Set expectations high. Accept no less than your best effort. And never give up!*
*FINALLY, PLAY LIKE A CHAMPION!*

toward the board and find out what their *"Do Now"* assignment is for the day. They sit down and start their *"Do Now"* assignment while I finish greeting kids at the door and take attendance.

That's how we start every single class. That's our routine. It's orderly. No one is just sitting there doing nothing. No kids are out of control in my classes. Well, usually there are no kids out of control. After all, kids are kids, and I think all teachers understand this disclaimer. But, all joking aside, the out of control behavior is not part of the routine, so it usually doesn't occur.

We have the same routine every single day. Why? Because kids crave that structure. Kids crave a routine. Kids crave that safety. Kids crave a certain amount of certainty. And… most of them don't even know they have these cravings.

Why do kids crave routine? Well, let's go back to that primitive mind again to prove my point that kids crave routine and structure. Imagine we're cavemen or cavewomen back in those primitive days, and we're running from sabre-tooth tigers. Now, it wouldn't be too far of a stretch to say that we humans want safety, right? We really do want to know what's going to happen next. We don't like walking down some path and not knowing what's going to happen. It's kind of scary not knowing what's going to pop out of the bushes at us, wouldn't you agree?

Our prehistoric ancestors craved for a routine so that they could hopefully anticipate what was going to happen next. Knowing what was going to take place was a good thing for our ancestors. It's in our DNA…Our students, even the ones that don't seem all that primitive, crave routines. It's a safety thing. Sadly, many of them are not getting these routines at home. The truth is kids like structures and routines. Trust me; they like that stuff. Routine, routine, routine. It works, and it's going to help us have fewer behavior problems in our classrooms.

Here's the deal. When the students come into class, through the use of routines, they already know what they are expected to do. We don't have to argue with them about doing the class work because this is what we do every single day. When they whine, we can blame it on the routine, like this:

"Hey, don't get mad at me buddy. It's just part of the routine. That's what we do every day. You come into class, and you do what you have to do. It's just the routine. You know this. We do this every day…" and that's all I got to say about that. Don't you simply love that phrase from Forrest Gump? ?

*Chapter Eleven*

# Be Interesting

Here is another thing to think about as a teacher. Some of you might disagree with me on this one, but, as a teacher, you have to find ways to become more interesting to your students. I can already hear some of you saying, "Hey! What the heck do you want me to do? Should I just set myself on fire or something like that! Setting myself on fire might be one of the few things these kids will actually pay attention to after playing all those shoot 'em up fire 'em up video games."

Please don't set yourself on fire. I don't want any of you doing that sort of thing to be interesting. Besides, setting yourself on fire hurts terribly, and you can probably only do that once. It's not a sustainable teaching methodology. Nah… Don't do that fire thing. We need some strategies to make us more interesting to our students that are sustainable and capable of being repeated. Besides, why would you set yourself on fire when I'm going to offer you some things that are a lot less painful and much more doable?

Trust me. These ideas are good stuff. It's going to be awesome. You're going to be awesome! You're going to love it. Plus, you're going to become more interesting, as well as a better teacher.

I want all you teachers out there, right now, to think about some things that you wanted to do that you haven't done yet. If you're having trouble thinking of something, then I want you to go back, go way back, go all the way back to your youth, and start there, okay? When you were still young and naïve and thought you could conquer the world, what were some of the things you wanted to do?

Was it to ski down a mountain? Was it to run a marathon? Was it to go kayaking down a waterfall? Was it to start your own business? Start your own podcast? I know… I know… podcasts didn't exist back then, but you know what I'm trying to say here. I'm talking in the language of our deferred dreams. Notice I said deferred dreams and not denied dreams. Even we, teachers, can still achieve our dreams! The remarkable and fantastic thing about our dreams is that it isn't selfish either. Seeking and achieving these personal goals make us better teachers too. I know you secretly want that particular thing you used to dream about but have buried deep in your psyche. I'm going to permit you to dream about it again and help you get it, okay?

I know that we, teachers, are natural martyrs who give up our own dreams to help others achieve theirs. But, the truth is, we don't have to do that anymore. We really can have our pie and eat it too when it comes to getting our dreams while helping others achieve theirs.

Come on… Work with me here. What is something that you wanted to do when you were thinking about ruling the world, but you haven't done yet? Believe it or not, you still have a chance to achieve your dreams. Well, maybe not rule the world, but you sure can do that other thing you used to think about when you still wanted to rule the world. Just do it. Come on… Was that other thing to join a gym? Was it to learn how to box?

Imagine yourself strutting into class one morning, and you share how you had a good workout yesterday in the gym. Kids like hearing that stuff, you know. Think about it. They might even think, "That teacher is crazy… but interesting." Yup. Interesting. They'll think, "She boxes? Dang! Maybe I shouldn't mess with her." They may even ask you if you have ever punched somebody in the face. You'll answer, "I sure have! I punched this huge guy right in the face last night during boxing practice."

Be interesting! Figure it out! What was that special something you always wanted to do but have been deferring until now? Still can't think of something? Then go and ask your siblings, your parents. Ask anybody who was around and knew you when you were still very young and hopeful.

Maybe you'll take up skiing again. Maybe you'll go skydiving. Maybe you'll go rock climbing. Maybe you'll start your own little business. Maybe you'll braid hair in the Bahamas as your summer job. I don't know what you'll do, but you'll do something, alright? Something! Do you know what's beautiful? While you're doing something interesting, you can share it with a rather large audience because now it's reasonably affordable to have your personal web page. How's that for a deferred dream? You can post on social media about how you rock climb, go cliff diving, rescue dogs, do this, do that, and do all that great stuff. That's speaking your students' language, isn't it? You are now, in reality, becoming more interesting to your students, aren't you?

Hey, I know we have to be careful about sharing too much stuff with our students, but I'm sure with some common sense that you'll figure out where the line is. Eventually, people will be talking about how they saw a super cool video on social media of you kayaking down a waterfall, or boxing, or whatever it is that you love to do that you have been putting off until now. Maybe you'll even overhear some students in school say, "You should have seen her knocking around her opponent in the ring.'" That would be totally cool, wouldn't it?

Be interesting! Now listen, I already know some of you will say, "It's not my job to be interesting. My job is to teach English."

I have to be honest with you. I giggle a little bit every time I hear teachers say, "I teach English," or "I teach math." Do you want to know what I say to those teachers? "Really? Because I teach kids English, and I teach kids math." Believe it or not, it is that easy of a transition to flip this kind of faulty thinking, based solely on content, onto its head. We teach kids first and content second. In other words, we don't need to teach content because the content is content. We can't teach it more content—we can only teach kids content.

Listen, all playing with words aside, I know it's very important to teach content. I know it's very important to know your content exceptionally well. I love the subject material. I love being an expert on some subject matter. Nevertheless, while content is necessary, the bottom line is that it's not everything. It's the kids who matter most. The kids have got to come first.

We have to get good with the kids. Next, we get good with the content. In all honesty, doing well with both the kids and the content is completely cool. You can throw interesting little, content tidbits into the class and get the kids to laugh, to think, or to become off guard. If both the content and instruction are interesting, we can make our students laugh and learn, which will help our students to like and respect us more. Heck, they may even want to be similar to us someday. What a compliment that is and what a testimony that is to us as people and educators!

Hey, speaking of that, does anybody know what the last thing Teddy Roosevelt said to President-elect William Howard Taft back in the early 1900s?

Picture this. Teddy Roosevelt wanted to get out of D.C. after Taft's inauguration in order to go on a big game hunting in Africa. He loved that sort of thing, you know. Does anybody know yet what the last thing he said to Taft when he was leaving? You ready for this? Are you truly ready for TR's sage advice to Taft? Here it is: He said, "Whatever you do, stay off the horses." Taft was 350 pounds! That's funny, isn't it? Taft is expecting some great parting advice from his dear friend and mentor, and the last thing Teddy says is, "Whatever you do, stay off the horses."

Of course, we can't forget about the Ronald Reagan story. Many years later there's that Presidential story of Ronald Reagan with the Queen of England and something about passing gas... I won't spoil that one for you. I'll let you research it on your own so that you can get a real deep, belly laugh... Oh, by the way, William Bennet, Drug Czar and former U.S. Secretary of Education, personally told me this story about Reagan. The story is in his book. If you want to look it up, you can become that interesting content expert who our students need these days. You can be that same person who stands right beside them, loves them, protects them, and cares for them as people.

You see, throwing in little tidbits of interesting and funny content catches our students' attention. Because it catches them off guard and by surprise, you get them to laugh and like us more. If they smile, giggle, and laugh, we now have them closer to being on our side. Believe it or not, we're entertaining them. Entertainment is what they do and what they consume. They entertain themselves all day long on those video games and social media. They come to our classrooms, and you're going to tell me that we're not going to try to entertain them at least a little bit? Hmm… I disagree… We have to entertain them at least a little bit. It's just the way things are nowadays.

Hang on. Hold on. I know what you're thinking. I say, "Don't give me that garbage about you're a teacher and not an entertainer." The truth and reality are that you are both an educator and an entertainer. For example, remember when we talked earlier about the psychology of sales and how it helps teachers sell their products which are themselves, their content, their class routines, and management procedures? Well, some of you are probably still thinking, "I'm a teacher, not a salesman." Once again, the truth is that you are an educator, and a salesperson, and an entertainer.

Have you ever thought or heard this one? "I'm a teacher, not a psychologist." You're both. What about this one? "I'm a teacher, not their parent." You're both. Lastly, this one? "I'm a teacher, not a judge." You're both. You have many, many hats to wear as a teacher in today's classrooms. You do all those things and more. You do whatever is necessary as a teacher to get your students to succeed. Entertain them, be interesting, and learn your content as best as you can. Look for a few funny and interesting tidbits buried deep in that content. Those entertaining tidbits will make your students giggle and help them feel more connected to you.

Let me ask you again. What are some things that you wanted to do that you haven't done yet? What are your deferred dreams? Really? Hmm… That actually might be kind of interesting… and fun… I wonder what the kids will think of it. I bet you that they'll think the content is kind of cool, and I bet that they'll think that you're cooler now too!

Maybe we, teachers, should travel more and then share these experiences with our students so we can see that remarkable look of awe in their eyes. Wouldn't that be amazing? Special? Maybe we should show up somewhere in their lives on a weekend wearing blue jeans. They can see us as more than a properly-dressed teacher who might be looking a little stuffy. Maybe we should eat out occasionally at a favorite local restaurant and then share this dining experience with the kids on the next day. Kids love talking about food and great local places to eat. Maybe we'll even bump into some of our students and break bread with them. That would be totally hip, wouldn't it? What's better than breaking bread? Please don't say what the Queen did with Ronald Reagan, okay? I've already heard that joke more times than I can count.

*Chapter Twelve*

# C.A.N.D.I

I use something else that helps my students want to like me more, trust me more, do business with me more, and do what I say more. This technique is something that I call the CANDI system. First, I put a CANDI sign right at the entrance of the door where they walk into class. They can't miss it! They can see and touch the CANDI sign. Second, I put another CANDI poster on the inside wall, right where they exit the room so they can see it and touch it. I put our CANDI signs in these locations to make it one of the first things students see and touch upon entering our learning zone (classroom) and one of the last things they see and touch when leaving our class, ready to go out there and take on the world.

These mini-posters are at eye level. The students can't miss them and thus are softly persuaded to think about them, at least on the subconscious level. These little signs are only one small part of my CANDI system. C.A.N.D.I. stands for Constant And Never-ending Deliberate Improvement. Our goal in my classroom is to continuously and deliberately improve a little bit, every day. Just a little bit every day, okay? That's all we need to achieve and to become more successful.

I always tell my students that by living this philosophy of improving a little bit on a daily basis, they'll find themselves within a couple of short years at a whole different level and a whole new place in their lives. They'll be in much better places in their lives. They'll be in places that are highly desirable.

Another component of my CANDI system is that I have them draw a CANDI logo on the top of their class work. The symbol consists of a circle or oval with two small triangles at the ends. Anyone can draw it, and it resembles one of those old-fashioned hard candies. CANDI is our class logo. The self-drawn CANDI logo on the top of all their papers helps the students to see and think about improving a little bit every day. What's more, anybody that sketches that small CANDI logo on the top of their paper gets one point of extra credit.

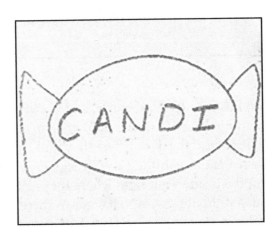

You wouldn't believe how easy it is to get most of the students to put this class logo on their papers. As a result, they think about its message and improve a little bit every day on an on-going basis! They merely draw logos on top of their papers every class, and then I give them that extra point they eagerly desire. This single point doesn't make much of a difference in their grades, but they think it does. This one extra point motivates them to do it! More importantly, that little symbol that they put at the top of their papers reminds the students of the class logo. As a result, they deliberately try to improve every day at least subconsciously. This reminder is essential!

Furthermore, they are also physically moving their bodies somehow by putting their pen to their paper solely to get that little point by drawing the class CANDI logo. They are not sitting there comatose. They have started their class work, and they don't even know it. Their efforts are also one of those little "yesses" that I will explain to you later in this book. Moreover, because they have taken the first step of putting their pencils or pens to their paper, we hopefully have some momentum, and I will have better success in getting them to complete their warm-up assignment that I call a "Do "Do Now." Importantly, the CANDI logo helps us all use the common vocabulary of constant improvement.

Every time they ask me about that extra point, I say, "Yeah Man. You get your point for drawing that CANDI logo for 'Constant And Never-ending Deliberate Improvement.'" I really do give it to them. I even put (1+) directly next to every CANDI logo they draw on their papers.

The next part of my CANDI system is that I make up CANDI awards that I hand out almost weekly. I recognize students' efforts and hang the awards up on the bulletin board. You too can make some CANDI awards tweaked to fit your style and the needs of your particular class. It's easy to do. The CANDI award applies to anything you want. For example, if your students have poor attendance, then you could make a CANDI award for attending school for ten days in one quarter.

Creating the awards is quick and easy with simple steps. First, take a little brown crayon and color the CANDI award brown. Next, we have a bronze CANDI award to hand out to any kid that comes to school for ten days. Maybe the challenge in your class is poor attendance and work completion. If it's appropriate, you make out a bronze CANDI award based on the student coming to school for ten days or more and for doing all of his or her work for ten days or more. It's simple and effective. Kids love it because they love getting prizes.

You might want to throw homework in there too. Maybe your criteria for the Bronze CANDI award becomes the students attending school for ten days or more, completing all their work for ten days or more, and doing all their homework for ten days or more. Perhaps, you want to create a Bronze CANDI award for kids who didn't have to go to the office or maybe didn't get a detention for ten days. The beauty of this technique is that you can implement it however you want and where ever you see the need in your class. You must be sure to make the CANDI award achievable. If only a few of the kids are earning the CANDI awards, then it will quickly lose its effectiveness.

As I mentioned before, the CANDI awards are easy. Merely take your little brown crayon and scribble all over the place on that CANDI award. It's fun! Go ahead, and try it. It's especially fun at the end of the day when you're worn out. You finally get to scribble like one of the reckless kids who you've been trying to hold in check all day long. Do another one with a grey crayon! We'll call this our Silver CANDI award. Even better, make another with yellow and call it the Gold CANDI award!

Let me explain to you a little bit more about how the system works. We have Bronze CANDI awards for any student that has ten or more of whatever we want them to do. We have Silver CANDI awards for any student that has twenty or more of whatever we want them to do. Lastly, we have Gold CANDI awards for any student who has thirty or more of whatever we want them to do per quarter.

Every once in a while we may experience a kid in our class who reaches forty or more of whatever we want them to do in a single quarter of the school year. It's possible. I've had it happen a couple of times over the years. In these instances, I leave the CANDI award blank. I make a big deal about it and announce to the whole class how this student earned a Platinum CANDI award. In front of everyone, I give that kid a box of crayons and tell them to scribble all over it. They are allowed to color it however they want and in any color that they want. Trust me! They can get pretty creative with these Platinum CANDI awards.

After I get the kids to put their names on their CANDI awards, I hang them up on a separate CANDI bulletin board. I have a special Bronze

CANDI section, as well as, Silver and Gold CANDI sections. Rarely do I need a Platinum section. If I do, then I find some room in the Gold CANDI area.

Sometimes, I even hand out gift certificates to go with the Gold CANDI and the very rare Platinum CANDI awards. You don't have to do certificates if you don't want to. Award systems can get quite expensive very fast for us teachers living on a limited budget. Customize awards and recognition in ways that are going to work for your class this year and do as many free things as you can, like these CANDI awards.

Comically, after a while, some of the students will ask, "Why did you scribble all over the CANDI awards? Why didn't you color within the lines?" I reply, "Well, besides it being lots of fun, I also did it to remind you all that life is messy, and education is messy sometimes. Learning isn't always neat and pretty and orderly. Occasionally, we have to think outside the box and color outside the lines to make our way in this world." Then I add, "Why did it take you guys four weeks to ask me that question?" That question really gets some of them thinking…

Hey, you want to know something? Just be creative and use this CANDI thing however you want to as long as it serves your purpose of improving student behaviors and academic performance. Use it in any manner that will make your kids better behaved and consequently make your teaching easygoing for you, okay? Experiment and have some fun with it. When it comes to classroom management, color outside the lines in your classroom.

I can already hear some of you clever ones saying, "Do they ever wonder if they are going to get the actual candy instead of CANDI?" My answer to that sweet-tasting question is that they sure do! I have kids asking me all the time, "Mister, can I get candy today?"

I respond, "Sure! I've got some candy with an 'I.' That's right. Candy with an 'I.'"

They whine, "Come on, Mister, you know what I mean."

I say, "Yeah! I know what you mean. You mean candy with an 'I.'"

Hey, what can I say? I know kids love candy. I catch their attention by talking about candy but give them candy with an "I" instead, which is once again Constant And Never-ending Deliberate Improvement. Go ahead and put that on the top of your paper, and I'll give you a 1+.

CANDI is only one of the things in my bag of tricks of teaching students to behave so I can be more successful with these difficult students and get them to do better in school. CANDI builds a better climate and better relationships, and it helps create some work ethic among my students. Sometimes, it can even help the students to feel better. I know because I see it when they all clap and smile when I hand out CANDI awards every Monday morning. Nice way to start the week, wouldn't you agree?

*Chapter Thirteen*

# Good Things

I'm guessing that since you're a teacher and an adult that you probably already know a little something about psychology. Do you remember hearing somewhere that the first thing you hear and the last thing you hear are the things we tend to remember best? I'm sure you do. We learned this rule of psychology in our teacher preparatory programs, right? That's why we, teachers, always try to have a good opening, initiation, hook, or whatever they want us to call it these days to begin teaching our lessons. Likewise, we plan for a strong closing, closure, or exit slip, or whatever they want us to call it these days to end our lesson.

Well, I too try to use that first and last law of psychology by making sure that I have a dynamic opening and a dynamic closing for my class. I'm sure a lot of you do the same thing. However, let me tell you about how I build powerful and unique openings and closings into my routines for my students that encompasses more of a holistic approach to developing the whole child.

If there is one thing I want my students to remember the most, it's that they like being in my class more than they like skipping my class or just being somewhere else. According to the laws of psychology, the stuff they hear from me in-between my grand and unique opening and fantastic closing will be a little harder for them to remember. Nevertheless, I'm not sweating that very much because I know that if my story-telling and content are exceptionally good and I've taken the necessary time to build relationships, then I'll get most of the kids to remember something about the middle of my classes as well. After all, I bet you still can remember how Teddy Roosevelt told Taft to stay off the horses as his sage departing advice during Taft's inauguration, right? That tidbit was hidden deep in this book, wasn't it?

You must be wondering what these unique beginning and closing routines are that I am alluding to here. Part of the beginning routine for my classes in some way has already been shared with you earlier. However, there is still more to it, and I will tell you what that is right now.

Here it is. Another part of my routine that begins my class is an activity that I call, "Good Things."

If you remember from previous chapters, this is the routine that I start all my classes. First, students encounter me saying hello to them when they enter my room. They shake my hand. Boom! They slap the Class Creed right where it displays, "Play Like A Champion." They enter the classroom and look at the board for their assignment. They sit down and start their "Do Now" assignment.

Next, I take attendance while they're working. I don't call out names or ask the class where certain kids are. That only disrupts them, gets them off-task, and gets them talking about other things. I quietly take attendance, and before they know it, I'm circulating the class like a quiet, stealthy ninja teacher that came out of nowhere. I'm nowhere and everywhere all at the same time.

Eventually, I come out from the midst of them and make my way to the front of the class. Guess what? Believe it or not, I don't even ask them what's the answer to number one is. Nope! That's not what I do. Instead, I vigorously read the greeting I already have written on the board that says, "Happy Monday, my young, awesome, aspiring historians!"

They yell back, "Thank You!" (I taught them to say, "Thank you.").

I continue by saying, "Okay, who has some good things?"

That's how we start all my classes. I get goosebumps every day doing it. Even thinking about it right now as I am writing this sentence, I get goosebumps running up and down my spine. Can you feel it? Try this routine, and you might get them as well.

Here it is. I'm still not asking anyone what number one is from the "Do Now" assignment. I'm asking, "Who's got something good to share with us today?"

"Come on… I need at least three students to tell me something good. What have you got that's good?" I bellow out to the class.

If nobody raises their hands, then I pick someone and say, "Thank you for volunteering, Jose!" or whatever their name is…

They usually look at me weird and say, "But, I didn't volunteer."

I completely ignore this and ask him again, "What's good today, Jose? What's your Good Thing?"

He seems stunned and replies, "I got nothing good."

"Oh, are you sick?" I ask him.

Again, he looks at me with a funny expression and says, "I'm not sick."

That's when I respond, "Good! That's your Good Thing. You're not sick. You're healthy."

I carry on my prowling through the class. "How about you? What's your Good Thing, Angel? And, thank you too for volunteering, Angel."

Angel laughs and replies, "I didn't volunteer."

I ignore his comment and say, "What's your good thing, Angel?"

Angel responds, "I got nothing."

I ask, "Are your shoes dry?"

Angel says, "What?"

I ask again, "Are your shoes dry?"

He says, "Dry?"

"Yeah. Did you step in the creek today on the way to school and get your shoes all wet?" I ask.

He spits back in disbelief, "No, I didn't step in no creek," again looking at me like I'm weird.

I completely ignore the looks and say, "Good! Well then, that's your Good Thing. Your feet are still dry."

After a while, the students begin to understand this game I play with them every day, and they even start to enjoy and participate in it. Sometimes, a kid will say, "Yo, Mister, I ain't' got anything good today, only a bad thing."

"Okay." I respond, "How 'bout you tell me what your bad thing is, and then I'll somehow turn it into a Good Thing."

They never seem to think that I can do this which encourages them to participate in the exchange with me. The kids tell me how they woke up late for school today and didn't have any time to eat, or something like that.

I immediately throw back a response that goes roughly like, "Your Good Thing is that you did wake up today, and soon you'll be eating lunch. See, look at that. You do have a Good Thing!" This exchange is how I open up every single class, every single day. When I finish getting Good Things out of at least three kids, I'll ask, "Who's got number one?"

To be candid, I did not make up Good Things. I want to think that I'm smart enough to have made this one up, but, I didn't. I stole this little strategy of "Good Things" from Flip Flippen of the Flippen Groups. No! I didn't say, "F- ing groups." I said, "Flippen Groups."

You see, many years ago I went to Flip Flippen's professional development called, "Capturing Kids' Hearts" and learned this activity there. I literally stole "Good Things" from Flip. I'm hoping that you're going to now steal it from me, the guy who took it from Flip Flippen. Hey, it's only fair, right? What goes around comes around, right? Go ahead and take it from me and use it in your class. I deserve that, don't you agree? I had it coming for a long time anyway, right? Do it!

Okay, all joking aside now, and the beauty of it all — Good Things — is that it only takes more or less two minutes to get three Good Things out of our students. The even more beautiful thing is that after a while you start to see students' hands going up on their own for this part of the class. That's a good thing, wouldn't you say? This response is one of those little yesses. This activity is building momentum, compliance, and habits. Anytime that we can get student engagement, we make progress. That's how I start the class by weaving "Good Things" into my unique, class opening every day. Now that we finished that let me finally ask you, "Who's got number one?"

For the end...It's coming real soon. So soon, it's coming next, in the next chapter...

*Chapter Fourteen*

# The Blessing

Are you ready for what's next? Or maybe I should say what's last. I end every class with my students in a freaky, bold way. I call it, "The Blessing." It's not a religious thing or anything like that. Come on people… I am a former history teacher. I know all about that whole separation of Church and State thing.

"The Blessing" started in section 158 of the free public library which is the applied psychology section. Here's the deal. According to the psychology books that I read from section 158 in our free public libraries, what our children hear before they go to bed at night gets programmed into their subconscious mind. Without even realizing it, they think about these thoughts while they're sleeping. I figured I would try to program my children for happiness and success by saying loving and empowering things to them right before they went to sleep.

After reading them their bedtime story, I'd sit there on the side of their beds with my hand on each one of my kids' hearts and recite "The Blessing" to them before they went to sleep every night. I wanted what every good parent wants—our kids to feel protected, happy, successful, and well-adjusted. I wanted this even if that meant trying something as innovative and outside the box of normal thinking as programming my children for this success and happiness. Then… I prayed that it worked.

I wanted my kids to know that their daddy loves and protects them and that they are special, and capable. I wanted them to believe, at least subconsciously, that they are wearing a coat of armor that will protect them, a coat of protection made from "The Blessing" and their daddy's love and encouragement. I wanted them to genuinely know and feel that everything was going to be okay no matter what.

The last words I said to them before they went to sleep every night, hopefully, would work on their sub-conscious minds and help them wake up feeling good about the new day and their place in this great big, exciting world. When my children woke up, they probably didn't know why they felt good, but they did feel good. That was good enough for me.

I carried out this blessing with my kids for years, and suddenly, one day I wondered why I wasn't doing the same thing with my students. I thought that it could be the last thing I say to my students as they leave my class. Still, this seemed a little scary to me. It's one thing to give my children "The Blessing," but a whole other story to give it to my students, right?

My students are probably going to think that I'm a really weird dude if I attempt to do this, I thought. Well… I did it anyway. I faced my fear and did it anyway because I knew my students deserved it and needed it. At first, they did look at me like I was quite weird. But… after receiving "The Blessing" a few times, my students began to warm up to it. Some of my students even came close to happy tears on a few occasions. Some of them brought in their moms during the parent-teacher night, and they told their moms that they wanted me to be their daddy because of "The Blessing."

Imagine that? These high school girls wanted me to be their daddy. These are high school girls! Not second graders! But, high school girls! I figured "The Blessing" must be working, and I decided to keep doing it, even though it was still kind of weird and extremely unconventional. I kept trying to program my students more and more for happiness and success because more is better, right?

I was ardently trying to program them for success. I believed that when my students left the classroom, it's not always going to be very enjoyable for them out there. That's why I tried to put a subconscious coat of armor on them by giving "The Blessing." I wanted them to feel loved, protected, and capable when they do go out there on their own. Hey, they're going to have to go out there eventually because they can't stay in my room forever, even if they want to. After all, what will their mothers think if they tried to stay here in my classroom forever?

The bottom line is that through "The Blessing" my students leave my classroom every school day and enter into the real world where hopefully they now feel protected, safe, respected, and capable. I want them to journey out to the real world with some pride and a coat of armor to protect them from all the piercing arrows and mudslinging from others. With any luck, their coat of armor that I programmed in them through "The Blessing" doesn't get too worn down before they get back to me the next school day.

The funny thing here is that, after a while, my students fell in love with "The Blessing." In fact, if I'm running behind schedule and it looks like I might not be able to squeeze in "The Blessing" before the bell rings, they insist, "Hey, Mister, you gotta do 'The Blessing.'" Can you believe that? Can you believe that they always stay, even if the bell rings in the middle of my hurry-up version of "The Blessing" when I'm running late?

You're probably wondering what is "The Blessing." I'm glad you asked and here it is.

*I say: "You guys got big hearts, strong bodies, and powerful minds. I feel*

# Mr. Blanchard's Blessing

*You have big hearts*

(Put your right hand on an imaginary heart)

*A strong body*

(Move your right hand right to an imaginary bicep)

*And a powerful mind*

(Move your hand up to an imaginary head)

*I feel your heartbeat*

(Complete the circle by moving hand down to imaginary heart)

*And I know this world is a better place because you were born*

(Put your hand on your own heart)

*Your teacher loves your forever and ever; no matter what!*

*So today when you go out in that world*

*my princesses and princes of New England;*

*go out with bravery and courage!*

*You have been blessed*

*You have been armed*

*You are strong*

*And you can handle anything that the world throws at you*

*today*

*Ain't that right…*(say a student's name)*…?*

*your heartbeats, lub-dub-lub-dub-lub-dub,"* (They like that part.) *"And the world is a better place because you were born. Your teacher loves you forever and ever and ever, no matter what. So, today, when you go out in that world, my princesses and princes of New England, go out with bravery and courage. You have been blessed. You are armed, you are strong, and you can handle anything that this world throws at you today. Ain't that right Angel?"*

Angel often shares, "Yeah!"

I say, "Ain't that right, Gabe?"

Gabe replies, "Yeah."

"Ain't that right, Anthony?"

Anthony also responds, "Yeah."

I get them all pumped up so when they go out there, and someone says to them, "Dude, you really freaking left your house wearing that shirt today?" Hopefully, these insults bounce off their coat of armor that I just gave them with "The Blessing."

Because I believe it's my job to create an excellent place, climate, and environment within the four walls of my classroom that gives all of my students a chance to succeed inside and outside the four walls of my room, I'm willing to try anything that will program my students for success and happiness. I'm eager to attempt and armor them with "The Blessing" in order to protect them as best as I can. When the class is over, I want all the junk out there to bounce off of them until they can get back to me tomorrow. Then, I can bless them all over.

It's all part of creating that unique climate and those valuable relationships that I talked about earlier. Believe it or not, "The Blessing" fits nicely into our class routine because it only takes approximately thirty seconds. After many years of having "The Blessing," students come back and ask, "Hey, Mister, do you still do "The Blessing?""

You bet I do! Regardless of how weird it may seem… Go ahead and sell this educational benefit to your students.

*Chapter Fifteen*

# Positive Postcards

Another great strategy or tool I use to build that positive climate and those great relationships in my classroom with my students is Positive Postcards. My school is a big help here because they supply the postcards and pay for the postage. I don't spend a penny. Isn't that great? I just put the kid's name and address on one side, a few kinds and supportive words on the other side, and drop it into the wire out-going box in my school's main office.

I keep the postcards short, simple, and sweet. I may scribble something such as, "Hey, Jose, great job today! Loved the way you lent a pencil to one of your classmates." Or, I may write, "Great job asking questions in class today, Billy." I end every postcard on a positive note with my signature closing of, "Keep up the good work and keep smiling!" I drop it in the main office box, and they mail it out. It doesn't cost me a dime. Nor does it cost me much time. It's easy, efficient, and effective.

These positive postcards help me keep all of my students on my radar, not just the ones that are being a pain in the butt. You see, before I started using my Positive Postcard strategy, my radar was tuned in on the kids who were talking and not paying attention, as well as the ones who were misbehaving in other ways, or about to misbehave someway. Let's not forget about the kids who were not doing their work. I was zoning in on the perpetrators.

I couldn't help it. My radar was tuned or programmed into the difficult students before I started sending postcards to my students' homes. You can probably imagine that seeking out the negative behaviors all day exhausts us, teachers. Nowadays, my teacher radar has been reset to the kids who are doing something nice or good because I need to send someone, anyone, a postcard today. At the beginning of each class, I don't know to whom I am going to send my daily Positive Postcard. Regardless, I have to find someone to send one. I better get looking!

Through this Positive Postcard strategy, I have forced myself to look for and to find the good in kids, instead of focusing on what they're doing wrong that's annoying me. After all, I do need to send a postcard every day. That's why I really do need to find somebody today and every day. The cool thing about this strategy is that it changes our view of our students and what we actually see in our classroom. If we send out a Positive Postcard every single day, and maybe even two or three every single day, then by Christmas, almost every one of our students would have received a postcard from us, even if we have 150+ students.

I also track who I send postcards to by putting a little mark next to their name on a clipboard I secretly keep on my desk. I do this to avoid sending one kid, who is outstanding, twelve postcards and ten kids who are… you know what… ahhh… not so awesome… none. On a regular basis, I look at my class list and the little marks next to my students' names to see who I still need to send a Positive Postcard.

When I notice someone who hasn't gotten one yet, like little Ricky, I'm thinking that little Ricky has been driving me crazy. Regardless, I have to find something good about him today in order to send him a postcard. Oh! There it is! Little Ricky just put his name on his paper. I'll send out the postcard that night to little Ricky for putting his name on the paper. I try especially hard to make sure that I send every student of mine a postcard by Christmas. Before the year is over, every kid gets two, three, four, or even five postcards.

I know. You're wondering if the students even care about the postcards, aren't you? My answer is yes. As a matter of fact, some of them are known to put the postcards up on their refrigerators. Some students take pictures of them and put those pictures up on Facebook and other social media sites. Some even bring them into school and show me the postcard I sent them with big a big smile on their faces.

Some are known to say, "Mister, yesterday my mom was screaming at me, and I was in trouble." I asked them, "Why?" My student replied, "Something came in the mail, and my mom started yelling 'What did you do now?' She looked closer at the mail and noticed it was a postcard that said, 'Ricky, you asked some great questions in class today, and you put your name on your paper too.' All of a sudden my mother was happy and giving me hugs. Thanks, Mister."

I already know that some of you are thinking that you can send this postcard digitally. Or, you can send an email, right? You can even send a virtual e-card, right? Well, that is true. While you can do those digital things, a paper postcard in their hands that came through the mail is somehow different, unique, and better. It's something they can hold. It's multi-sensory. It's something concrete they can be proud of receiving.

Our kids are getting digital things all day long. How many of our kids get a piece of mail. None of them ever do! They never get a piece of mail that they can physically hold in their hands. When they get this Positive Postcard in the mail, it's probably the only piece of mail they've ever gotten. It sticks. In return, they stick it on to their refrigerator. Like I said, "It really sticks." Many times that note is still up there years later. Yup… it's still hanging out there on their refrigerators, still sticking to its surface and their memories of our class and me together.

Want to know something cool, or something that could be really cool? I'm still waiting for one of my students to come to school someday and tell me that they saw their mom's or dad's postcard from me up on their refrigerator… Someday, if I teach long enough, I know it's going to happen. I can feel in my bones that it will happen.

When you send those postcards, don't address them to the students' parents. Address them to your students. Postcards are wide open and transparent. There's Jose's name nice and big right there on the postcard, and it says, "Good job in class today, Jose!" The postcard isn't closed up.

Consequently, mom can see clearly and immediately that her child is being praised. Remember, parents get mail, but our students never get mail. This positive gesture is impactful. Therefore, make sure you address the postcard to your student, not the parent.

If the mother does see it first and then flips it over, she can see that her child helped somebody in class today. He/she did his/her homework, or he/she did a good job writing an essay, or whatever good thing they did... Make the Positive Postcard out to the kid. It has way more impact when it's made out and sent to the student because the kid never gets mail. This part is very important to remember.

*Chapter Sixteen*

# Tie-Downs with Little Yesses

I read widely. I read all sorts of educational books. I also understand all kinds of books on psychology, books on sales, and a whole bunch of other exciting and useful things. One day while I was reading extensively and wondering how I can tie new learnings into my classroom teaching practices, I came across this guy by the name of Tom Hopkins. He is one of those gurus who trains the sales professionals. He seemed interesting, and a friend who was with me told me he liked him. In addition to the books I already had, I picked up a couple of Tom's books as well.

Tom Hopkins talks a lot about Tie-Downs. The psychology behind Hopkins' strategy of tie-downs in getting people (like our students) to do what we want them to do (complete their classwork or at the very least behave well) is exceptionally simple and effective that I couldn't wait to try it out in my classroom on my students. I now use tie-downs all the time in my classes with my students. Hopkins taught me that tie-downs are as simple as using the same statements that we use every day in our daily teachings and merely attaching a little agreement question at the end. These little agreement techniques can also be in the beginning or even hidden in the middle.

Tie-Downs can be attached to practically anything we say. For instance, suppose we wanted to tell our students that George Washington was our first president. Psychologically speaking, we would be more effective teachers if we put a mini question after or before this statement.

An example might be, "George Washington was our first president, right?" (Tie-down at the end). Or, "Isn't it true that George Washington was our first President?" (Tie-down in the beginning.)

Do you see what's happening here? Don't sweat it if you don't know what the big deal is. If you're a bit lost, don't worry. You're still probably on the right track. Tie-downs are a very subtle technique for getting small agreements or tiny yesses that most of us would initially miss, and most likely, wouldn't truly understand the importance.

You see, the real beauty of tie-downs is that they help kids focus and become more agreeable. By the way, while I'm thinking about this, please get to know your students' names as quickly as possible and then attach them to your tie-downs for this technique to be even more effective. Also, any time a kid is mentally drifting away from paying attention to your lesson, you now have a useful tool to utilize to bring them back in a non-confrontational way quickly, don't you? Oh, look! That was a tie-down, wasn't it? Oh, isn't that another one of those tie-downs... Enough said.

Here's how it works. You see your student turning his back to you and talking to another kid. Maybe he's looking at you, but he's just not paying attention or perhaps doing something that he or she shouldn't be doing. Armed with a tie-down, all you have to do is lob a very easy statement with a tie-down attached to it. This technique in most instances helps you to get them back on task immediately without a fuss.

Another example might be that little Mary is drifting. Therefore, you say something elementary that all she has to do is nod her head to something like, "George Washington was our first President, right, Mary?" In a pinch, if you can't think of a quick statement to attach a tie-down to, you can say almost anything to get this kid back. For instance, "Lunch is at 11:30 today, right, Mary?" Bingo! Mary is back looking at you and paying attention to you, instead of amusing herself while you were trying to teach.

You see, I just got Mary back, or Ricky again, or whichever student was drifting away from me and my lesson. Little Mary, Ricky, or whoever is now looking at me and thinking about what I just said. He or she may even be thinking that maybe I like him or her because I just used his or her name and included him or her in the class conversation.

I do this all day long in my classes. All day long I'm talking to my students saying, "Isn't it true that…?" "This is what's happening, right, (name)?" "Would you believe…?" "You would agree with…?" Again, use their names with the tie-downs whenever possible and use this strategy all day long. It pulls the kids back to us in subtle ways that they don't notice. It's not threatening or confrontational in any way. It subconsciously builds stronger relationships because we're including them in our class conversations and getting little agreements from them. They are becoming more agreeable.

Teachers, have some fun with these tie-downs and use them to help you ramp up your emotional energy. Remember, emotion creates motion, right? If emotion creates motion, then it also creates energy, right? Hey, those were just a couple of tie-downs, weren't they? Oh, isn't that another one?

If we're having some fun with our students, we could teach forever, right? Well, let's have some fun with tie-downs and never get old, okay, teachers? Oh, that was just another tie-down that I used on you, wasn't it? Isn't it true that last question was just another one? We're having some real fun now, aren't we? I don't even have to say it, huh, teachers? You know what I'm doing to you now, don't you?

You see, the bottom line is that we have to be more dynamic than the kid next to the student we're trying to get to behave and learn. A tie-down is one more way to do that. If the kid next to him is more dynamic than we are, we're going to lose that kid to fooling around. He is going to want to hear what the kid next to him has to say more than he wants to hear what we have to say.

I don't know about you, but I don't want this happening in any of my classes. I'm always in the middle of my students (proximity) and using these little tie-downs as often as I can to get small yesses out of them. "Isn't that true, Dan?" "Wouldn't you agree with that, Gabe?" I'm getting tiny yesses all day long from my tie-down strategy. If you know the psychology of sales, little yesses help the ball to get rolling toward bigger yesses.

What are bigger yesses? Well, bigger yesses are things like, "Luis, I need you to take out your pen, okay, buddy?" You see, Luis taking out his pen is a bigger yes than Luis just shaking his head up and down to Washington being our first president. Other bigger yesses include such things as, "Mary, I need you to open your book," or "I need you to do some classwork, okay?"

You see, if I racked up a bunch of little yesses with Luis, Mary, and the rest of them, then when I'm looking for a bigger yes like "I need you to take out your pen," Luis, Jose, Gabe, Mary and the rest of them comply! They don't even know that they should comply by taking out their pens. They are beginning to believe that they should simply say yes. They're not sure why, but just saying yes and doing it seems reasonable. It's subtle. They don't even notice it, but we all know that little things add up to big things over time, don't we? Ah… Another one…

For example, if you're walking around the classroom and you notice little Bryan hasn't even started his classwork, instead of telling him to begin his classwork, you might now ask him to put his name on his paper so that he can get some class credit—a little yes! At the moment he may be unwilling to do his classwork, but he may think merely putting his name on the paper is okay. He's doing something that will probably help make you go away, which is what you do while he is writing his name on the paper.

Additionally, while I'm walking around checking on the other kids, I now notice that little Bryan has his name on his paper. His action is something that makes him subconsciously take some ownership in his paper, and he might start his classwork and continue with his writing. If not, I go to his desk again and ask him only to do number one. Ahh… Another little yes. Eventually, I'll build some momentum with these little yesses, and he'll probably do his work instead of getting in a good, old-fashion standoff with me at the O.K. Corral.

What I'm trying to say here is that if we're only reading educational stuff to enrich ourselves and improve our teaching practices, then I have some news for you. Are you ready? Here it is! Read more educational material! But remember, we can borrow from many other disciplines and areas that will make us better teachers. We can borrow from everywhere and anywhere that we can find something to help us help our students. It's all okay. Perhaps a little untraditional and a bit unconventional, out-of-the-box thinking is the secret to success with our difficult students…

Remember, little yesses add up to big yesses. We all want the big yesses, don't we? Oh, there goes another tie-down, huh? Hey, the bottom line is that we want our students to do the class assignment, behave, and be successful. If Tom Hopkins' Tie-Downs help us get tiny yesses that lead to bigger yesses, and if it helps us help our students in any way at all, then we should at least try it, right? Yeah… there's another, huh? I wonder how many little yesses I got out of you in this chapter.

*Chapter Seventeen*

# Storytelling

Are you ready for the next strategy for becoming more successful with difficult students? Yes! Well, good! Because here it is. Our following strategy for becoming more successful with difficult students is as simple as telling a story. Isn't that awesome? The beautiful thing is that every one of us can tell a story, and furthermore, every one of us can get increasingly better at becoming a remarkable storyteller!

I must admit I have a bit of an advantage over most teachers here in the storytelling realm because I spent a long time as a history teacher. History is full of amazing stories. Fortunately, I had a lot of opportunities to practice storytelling while I was teaching high school history for a decade.

Another advantage that I have is that I'm half Irish. You know the kind of stories the Irish can tell. Although… I'm coming right out now and telling you that I have never kissed the Blarney Stone, nor do I ever intend to have a story about kissing it. I've heard the stories about what some people have done to that piece of rock. My lips aren't going anywhere near that stone. As a matter of fact, I have never even been to Ireland, so those crazy stories about me and that stone can stop right now, please. Thank you.

The long and the short of it all is that my personality fits right into this concept or strategy of storytelling. Relating tales helps make my days with today's difficult students easier. This tactic helps me better manage the class. Because I am no longer a history teacher because of budget cuts, I'm now a special education teacher. (Some of you know the impacts of budget cuts!) My storytelling abilities assist me in running a calmer special education class that's more under control than it would have been otherwise. Even though my class is a behaviorally challenged class, some real learning is taking place, and some good behavior as well, despite their disabilities.

As a teacher, telling stories about successful people is quite easy because our students are still young and still think they can conquer the world by becoming one of those successful people. Our students want to be as well-to-do as the people in the stories. Tell them more stories! Regardless of what they may say to us, or how they may act contrary to being successful, they secretly really want that fame and fortune. They do want to know more about people who have achieved great things, and, actually, people in general. Why do you think reality television has become such a big hit? Kids love the storyline of people. They love gossip! They love stories!

Why is storytelling so effective? Well, it's because it takes us back to our primitive days. We are all hard-wired for storytelling. Relating narratives is the way we communicate. We primates, I mean humans, love to tell and listen to stories. Even if we lie and say we don't, the truth is that we do. We primates, I mean humans, love stories. As I said before, we are hard-wired for storytelling. Please remember that if someone says that they don't like stories, they're the ones telling a made-up story about not loving these entertaining sagas…

Let's get better at storytelling! How do we do that? Well, practice of course! Find a few teachable moments each day where you can tell a quick, informative, thought-provoking, or inspiring story. Don't worry. This telling can be done quickly and in only a few minutes which shouldn't take too much time away from your curriculum-pacing guide. It can enrich your curriculum and even speed up your curriculum pacing because you'll have more kids paying attention to their learning. You'll encounter fewer behavior problems once you get good at this teaching strategy.

Something that I've learned over the years is that today's kids are all over the place with their behaviors. Teachers can no longer pull out a lesson and think that the kids are going to sit quietly and behave for the next forty minutes. Teachers can no longer believe that students have the stamina to sit through one particular forty-five-minute activity.

That old teaching strategy no longer works well in education. Today's kids don't have the attention span or endurance to hang in there for the next forty-five minutes on one activity. Today, dividing our forty-five-minute classes into three fifteen-minute learning chunks helps to involve our students in three different activities. Fortunately, this structure is also good for storytelling.

For example, the first fifteen minutes we're doing this, Activity A. For the next fifteen minutes we're doing that, Activity B. Finally, for the last fifteen minutes we're doing those, Activity C. You get my drift on this chunking thing? Furthermore, we can also break up those fifteen-minute chunks by throwing in some quick stories here and there. The trick is to keep the class moving fast and to sneak in interesting stories wherever we can. The kids don't have time to get off task and fool around.

Hey, as I said, kids love stories. We do too! That's just the way it is. If you can get your students to be quiet and pay attention by listening to stories, then why not use this technique whenever you can? Who knows? Maybe one day, an administrator will walk into your class during one of your stories and be astounded, "Wow, you had them, man. You really had them. I've never seen a class before where I saw every single student focused on the teacher for the entire time like I did observing you today. Way to go, bud! You were a rock star up there in front of that class."

Amazing! Your administrator's positive and enthusiastic feedback really can happen when you have your students fully engaged in one of your great stories. I know this because it happened to me... but you want to know what's better than this happening to me during my storytelling? Where the child falls academically on the intellect or experience spectrum doesn't matter. Every student can pick up the story right where they presently are and get something from it. ***How's that for differentiation instruction! Bang!***

*Chapter Eighteen*

# Sharing

Remember in kindergarten when we learned to share? Well, believe it or not, this next strategy is going to be difficult for many of you. Even so, to struggle is good, right? Struggle builds the muscles big and strong with erect backbones, right? Trust me. This struggle is going to be good for you and good for your students. Do you believe me, yet? Good. Here we go. I want you to pick something that you've struggled with and share it with your students.

Doing this shows your students that you are human and not just that monster of a teacher who the kids are always looking at all weird. You see, sharing with your students is good, within boundaries of course. Sharing like we were still in kindergarten helps us build better relationships with our students.

Trust me! Sharing is going to make you and your students better. Pick something that you've wrestled with in the past and presently want to kick its butt. The struggle can be anything you want. If you still feel awkward about this and don't want to share something personal, then pick some general goal that you would like to accomplish. Tell the students about it. Share with them what you plan to do over the next year to move toward reaching your new goal.

Share it with them. Say something like, "Hey, everyone. Since I want each one of us in this class to improve in some area of our lives, I'm going to lead by example with an area of my life that has been giving me some trouble. Over this next school year, I want to accomplish this or that, or whatever..."

Maybe you want to write a book. Perhaps you want to give a speech without dying up there on that stage. Maybe lose ten pounds, whatever... It doesn't matter what it actually is, just as long as it is something. Don't worry. Anything... Any kind of goal will be fine. I don't care what it is. Tell them that you want to run across the country like Forest Gump if that's what you really want to do. I always thought, "Now that would be cool!" Listen and trust me. Pick something and then share it with the kids. Tell them that you need their help. That's right. You need their help.

They're going to look at you like you're crazy. Your students may even wonder, "Why the heck do you need my help? After all, you are the teacher, and I'm just the student?" They'll think that no other teacher has ever asked for their help before, especially with something that is special or personal to them.

You see, the psychology behind asking them for help is, believe it or not, that once someone asks for your help, you can't help but like them a little bit more. Furthermore, you won't even notice that you enjoy your students a little bit more, but you do. That means that your students will like you more... It's subtle, it's effective, it's easy, and it's awesome!

Say it! Come on... just like Sam Kinison in the movie, "Back to School," with Rodney Dangerfield during that lecture about the Vietnam War. Just say it! Just say it! Just say it! Okay, here it is: "Hey guys, I need your help. I need you to be my support group. I need to have somebody who will hold me accountable, so I can do better and be happier about life."

Then, tell them whatever your goal is or whatever it is that you've been struggling with over the years. Say something like, "I've been trying to get my mile run down to under ten minutes, and I just can't seem to do it. I've been trying hard, and I simply can't do it. I need to hold myself accountable to somebody who will help me do it. I need that someone to be you guys because now you guys are my students, which means now we're family. You guys are going to be my accountability group because we're like family here. Got it? Family! Now, you guys are going to be my support group, okay? Thanks, everyone."

Schedule a daily, weekly, monthly, or other convenient time, and quickly check in with your students. Let them know how you're doing. If you're human, like most of us, you're going to have some ups and downs in accomplishing your life goals. Hopefully, though, over the long run, you'll have more ups than downs, and you'll feel better about your progress.

Furthermore, your students will get to see what it's like to witness their teacher fail, and then pick him or herself back up and keep going. They'll see what it's like to watch their teacher have some ups and downs, lose some battles, but in the end, win the war. Witnessing this process of struggle and improvement in their teacher is very motivating for them. The students gain hope that they can do something like this and that they can accomplish some of their goals.

Be honest with yourself and your students though. Because if you are, I guarantee you this is what's going to happen. You're going to come in sometimes, and you're going to have to tell your students that you screwed up—you fell short of your goal. You're going to have to say to them the painful truth that you overate last night if losing weight is your goal. You're going to say something like, "We went out to dinner last night, and there was nothing healthy there to eat. I know that's just an excuse, and I screwed up, and I came in today a pound heavier than I was yesterday..."

Tell them that you're glad that you have them as your support group. Tell them that if it weren't for them, you probably would have been even worse. You'd probably be two pounds up, instead of one. The damage was smaller because you were thinking of them and tried to show some self-discipline. Tell them that you knew that you would have to tell them today about last night's overeating, and this morning's horror story on the scale. Tell them that they saved you from something much worse because you were thinking about them, your support group.

Tell them that they are your accountability system. Keep throwing encouraging kinds of words such as accountability at them. Keep saying things like, "You guys keep me accountable; you guys are my support group. You guys help me have more self-discipline because you help me behave more responsibly and productively while chasing my goals and dreams."

Share all of this with them. Hopefully, your life will improve, and you'll begin to think… "Dang, I didn't know I could really run a mile in under ten minutes or get back to my old college weight!" or whatever it is that you desire. You might think, "I never thought I could, in all honesty, write a book, I was only messing with the kids. I never thought I could, if truth be told, do it…" But… the next thing you know, you did do it. You did kayak down a waterfall. Hey, the cool thing here is that you get to feel a little better about yourself and your actual abilities, and you'll also find that you are self-empowering yourself. You now have more energy to teach all these little kids. Well, they're not all little. I know a bunch of them are already taller than I am… But, you know what I mean here… Hey! Hey! Stop making short jokes about me over there in that corner, buddy.

This experience is true! You did hear me correctly when I said that you'd have more energy to teach your students. Listen, not only will you have more energy, but you'll get to feel good about yourself and become more enthused about your teaching, your class, your students, and the bonds that you have created with them too.

You're throwing your dream list at them, and you keep reinforcing words like "accountability," and "you guys are my support group," and "you guys keep me self-disciplined." Now, when you throw it back in their direction and say, "Listen, I'm here to support you in getting your homework done every night," your statement is finally going to have a little bit of a kick to it. Achieving together is finally going to begin to register with them. Support from each other is ultimately going to mean something.

When you say things like, "Hey, listen, I'm holding you accountable for doing your class work, just like you're holding me accountable for writing that book I have always dreamed of writing," the words like accountable, support, and self-discipline have a little bit of a boom to them. They have some impact now on how the students think and behave.

This kind of innovative teaching isn't taking place in a book though. We're teaching our students through real-life lessons that are right in front of them. They can all see these real-world lessons taking place every day between them and us. Our students can see us having small failures and small successes all the time. They see us fail, succeed, fail, succeed, succeed, succeed, fail and succeed and succeed on a weekly basis. They also know that we keep going and going. We don't give up, regardless of today's results. Kind of like our teaching them too, huh?

One of the reasons why we don't give up on our deferred dreams that have become our life goals during this school year is because we're afraid of what our students are going to say to us if we do give up. We don't give up because we don't want our students to think that we're quitters. No matter how many times we fail, we keep going. We don't give up, and eventually, our students see that our lives are getting better and better because we're not giving up.

Right in front of their own eyes, the students are witnessing the transformation of their teachers becoming higher quality people. Through our actions, we are teaching our students something that's invaluable; that something is called "habits of success." Our students aren't going to learn those habits in a book, but instead right alongside a book during our human interactions with them through our goals. We're a real-life lesson standing right in front of them every day. Eventually, we become their role models because ultimately, we get our students to think that they too can achieve success. Perhaps they do want to go through a wall for their teacher. Maybe they do want to grab life by the horns and become the master of their destiny...

*Chapter Nineteen*

# Use Humor

In my school, like most high schools, the kids' electronics are ubiquitous. As you already know, our students' electronics are everywhere. Getting them to put their electronics away or leave the devices inside their book bags, pockets, or desk isn't easy, is it? Imagine squeezing toothpaste out of the toothpaste tube. Good luck putting that away. We aren't putting it back into the tube, no matter how hard we try, huh?

Electronics pervades everywhere in our new digital world. We have squeezed electronics out of the tube, and there is no putting it back inside no matter how hard we try. The harder we work, the messier it gets with the students, and the more frustrated we become as educators. They're here to stay, and that's that, I guess. The question becomes, how do we go forward from here?

To start, the use of handheld devices is going to grow more and more prevalent as technology continues to improve and become a more prominent part of our lives. In the meantime, while most of our schools still have rules about the kids not having electronics out in class or they will get some consequence for it, I find one of the better ways to deal with these electronics! I use a little humor. Since my school doesn't have electronic pouches for the kids to store their phones during class time, I calmly walk up to them and quietly ask if they can order me a pizza with extra cheese and extra pepperoni. "I love pepperoni!" I tell them.

At that point, they look at me with a bizarre look on their face as I repeat, "Don't forget the extra pepperoni." The students tend to giggle and put away their electronics. No hard feelings. No power struggles. However, to be fair, I must admit that some put it away slower than others. I guess that's just life, isn't it? (Oh… there's another tie-down, huh?)

If I see a student dragging his or her feet too much while putting it away, I'll remind them that I want extra cheese. "Don't forget the cheese. I love cheese too," I tell them. They eventually catch on that I'm cutting them a break and trying to humor them. They usually do the decent thing and just put away their devices. This light-hearted exchange is a good thing because a power struggle at this point is often a bad thing for everyone involved, including the spectators.

Additionally…squabbling is not necessary. Let's not get into power struggles with our students when we can use a little bit of simple humor to solve the problem. No kid wants to hand over their cherished electronic device to the teacher. Things could get ugly here if we don't employ a little humor. We could very quickly find ourselves back at that dreaded O.K. Corral demanding their phone and closely watching their hands.

If we try hard enough, we can use humor throughout all our classes. It makes a lot of sense to use humor as much as we can. For example, sometimes when kids ask me to go to the bathroom, and I don't want them leaving the room again, I'll ask, "Why?"

They say, "I have to pee."

I say, "I have a Q."

They look at me weird and ask, "What?"

I reply, "What?" and then just stare at them like I'm confused.

They moan, "Come on, Mister, I got to pee,"

I repeat, "Cool, I got a "Q." Does anyone have an "R?"

They say, "What?"

I say, "What?" and then just stare at them again like I'm confused.

Then, we do the drill all over again until they realize that I don't want them leaving the room repeatedly. The kids plead, "Why?"

I respond, "X."

They say, "Why?" again with a puzzled look on their face.

I answer, "X," again.

They say, "What?"

I say, "Y."

They say, "Why?"

I rapidly fire off, "X, Y, Z."

They return, "What?"

I respond, "X, Y, Z, A, B, C, you know me..."

They surrender, "Forget it," and usually go and sit down. The students' friends in the hallway are going to have to wait until another time for them to sneak out of class...

I know you'll probably think that while I'm messing with them, what about the academics? Hey, don't you worry! I think academics are funny and humorous too just like the old warped episode of Abbott and Costello's "Who's on First" scene. I just starred in that scene in the above episode with my students while they were trying to get out of the room again by asking to pee.

Okay. Here's another way to use humor. This one includes academics as well. Every once in a while I'll explain some problem, and then they'll ask me to say that again. I'll say, "Okay, that again!"

They look at me, and some quietly laugh. Some sit there looking confused. Some...Well, you know how that goes. They're in their own world and don't even realize a joke took place. However, some kids are pretty smart, and they'll ask me differently by saying, "Hey, can you go over that again." In response, I'll put my paper on the floor and step over it a few times while telling them that I'm going over it again. Along with my wittiness, I'll ask if there are any more questions.

Using a little appropriate humor puts everyone on the same side and doesn't take time away from the academics. It's useful for building relationships with our students and getting them to do more work. If kids are having a good time in class, psychologists have found that their brains become more absorbent rather than when they dislike learning. Enjoyment causes them to learn more, quicker. Their minds suck in all sorts of information when they like our classes, and maybe they'll even want to go through walls for us now.

However, if kids aren't having fun in our classes, psychologists have shown that our students' brains (Yes. They do have brains. Yes. All of them have brains) become more rigid and deflect, reflect, or flex away any information attempting to enter their brains. Rigid brains are a bad thing. They can't learn in this state of mind, nor can they even listen to us when they're not enjoying themselves.

Skillfully using humor helps us to get our students to do more of the things we want them to do and helps us have fewer power-struggles with them as well. The kids doing more of what we want is a good thing because dealing with bad behavior is a bad thing. Conflict makes us have a terrible day. Sadly, however, lousy behavior from our students is becoming increasingly common which is also bad. This poor student behavior makes avoiding a bad day tougher which is no laughing matter... I hope that their poor behaviors aren't already entirely squeezed out of the toothpaste tube... If so, that would be bad, very bad, and very messy to try to get them to put those bad behaviors back inside that tube.

I guess the educators are going to have to come in and try to fix this mess too... and then not give us any credit for it, right educators out there? Hey, another tie-down, huh?

*Chapter Twenty*

# Be Weird

Believe it or not, being weird is a good thing. I'm not talking about being the kind of weirdo that we, teachers, used to laugh at and watch on all the old 1980s Revenge of the Nerds movies. I'm talking the kind of weird that catches your students' attention, gets them to stop what they are doing (off-task behavior), and gets them back on the right track.

The right track includes them looking at us, paying attention to us, and studying us to see what we're going to do next. Hey, what can I say? To get our students' attention, sometimes we, teachers, have to be weirder than the drippy-nosed kid sitting right there next to them. Besides, what educational value is there for a kid to sit there and watch another kid's nose run and wonder if that other kid even knows that his nose is running? Maybe, he's waiting to see what that other kid will do once he realizes his nose is running. Here's the deal… Our students are better off paying attention to us than watching some kid's nose drip. Wouldn't you agree? Tie-down!

What exactly am I talking about when I say teachers should be weird? I'm talking about the weird that might involve a teacher stopping right in the middle of an oral sentence or profound thought and silently walking over to the clock. With the strangest look, the teacher halts the lesson and stares at the clock as if they just heard the clock say something and are waiting for it to come alive. Now, that's weird.

Do odd behaviors like this, and eventually, the class will quiet down.

The off-task behavior will stop, and all the kids will look up at the clock as well as if it's going to do something crazy. As you're counting the seconds by pointing your fingers at the different second and minute hands of the clock, you turn and look at the now quiet and confused kids. Looking like you've had an epiphany, you say, "Wow! That was thirty-eight seconds."

The kids will ask, "What was thirty-eight seconds?"

You respond that it took them thirty-eight seconds to realize that they were off-task and not paying attention to the lesson or you. Ask them if that seems right to them while holding a certain lost look on your face.

Trust me, the kids won't know what to make of this bizarre behavior, but you'll have their attention again. You'll repeatedly get their attention in the future when you do weird things like this. Now that you got them to be quiet and a little off balance, you might as well return to your teaching. Likewise, if you lose them again, simply repeat doing something weird to make them stop what they're doing and look at you wondering what the heck is going on…

Do you want to know what is weird? It doesn't matter what you do to be weird—as long as it's legal and ethical. Be weird because it's different and it's something the students aren't anticipating. This odd behavior doesn't fit into their usual pattern of teacher behavior. Because their primitive survival mind is telling them that something might be wrong, it breaks their off-task thoughts.

They can't help but stop what they're doing and look at what you are doing when you're peculiar. Maybe you're doing something strange like standing on a chair, singing something, playing the air guitar while laying across your desk, or playing the drums on multiple student desks. Perhaps you're walking over to the phone that isn't ringing, picking it up, and having an imaginary conversation with the President of the United States. It doesn't matter what weird thing you do. Plan something that is weird and gains their attention.

Keep doing these weird things as long as it's legal and ethical. By doing bizarre things, you'll gain a much better command of your class and have a lot more success with your difficult students. You'll be laughing a little bit inside thinking, "Dang, that crazy weird thing worked!" Your students will be smiling more too, and that's a good thing. Remember those who laugh together stay together. Furthermore, you'll have better attendance because your students aren't going to want to miss the show—the show that you put on every day.

# PART FIVE

## WHAT IF IT DOESN'T WORK?

*Chapter Twenty One*

# Don't Argue

Do you want to know something? One of the best things we can do for kids who are difficult and are not buying into the whole climate and relationship thing that we're trying to create and sell to them is to just not argue with them. Our students will try to start an argument with us. If we don't engage in their scheme, they're going to look foolish arguing with no one... Eventually, they'll notice that they're arguing with no one...They will feel silly and stop arguing with no one because their classmates are looking at them all weird—this person who they don't want to hang out with after school. Here's the ironic part. Unlike us teachers, kids don't get to act all weird and still be liked by the other students.

Back to arguing. You see, the truth is that kids don't have any power at all! They have none! No power! It's the truth. None at all! Even though this generation of adults, which includes me, has led kids to believe that they have all the power and are entitled, they aren't. The kids that kids are taught two things: 1) kids are powerful, and 2) we, adults, are weak and helpless. The real truth is that we, adults, have all the power, and the kids have none.

We are the adults; they are the kids. It is that simple. We don't have to complicate things. Kids have no real power. Please, let's stop bowing to them and building up their hubris and entitlement. Besides, the adults who told kids that they have all this power were only joking with them. Kids, because their kids, didn't get the joke... They thought it was real.

They felt they had dominance over us adults… Isn't that funny? Tie-down!

I want you to see that the occasional borrowed power that kids have is engaging us adults in arguments. When it comes to power, that confrontational engagement is all they have—nothing more. That power isn't even real. It's fake, and it's built on quicksand. Furthermore, kids, at best, only have that second-rate, phony power when we give it to them. We give our students the upper hand when we forget that they have no real power.

Consequently, we plunge into an argument with them. Don't do it. Don't argue. We are the adults. They are the problematic, still-wet-behind-the-ears kids who don't know much besides how to disagree with us.

I know that it's not always easy to not argue with kids. I've been there. I know that they are very clever at getting under our skin. I also know that sometimes we get these freaking crazy feelings when dealing with the most difficult ones. Regardless, it's still our choice to have our adult superpowers rise and save the day. Or, do we choose to let our immature, crazy juvenile emotional feelings rule the moment and cause us to question our self-worth? No matter how difficult these kids are, it still doesn't change the fact that we have the power, and they have none. They're kids, and they haven't earned their power yet.

If we don't engage in an argument with them, they've got nothing. Really! They've got nothing! Okay, let me use proper English here. The kids don't have anything on us. Listen, I get it. We've all been there and done that. We are the adults, and we are the ones in power. It's now our turn. We had to wait a long time to be old enough for it to be our turn to have all this power. Let's not give away our super abilities, especially to kids who aren't old enough, are misbehaving, and don't deserve it anyway!

I guess the question now becomes, how do we not participate in arguments with troubled kids when they are being very difficult and getting under our skin? These little itches are making our skin prickly and irritated to the point that we feel like viciously scratching it off! Well, sit tight, and let me tell you how to do this without scraping so hard that you cause harm.

*Chapter Twenty Two*

# The Broken Record Technique

Have you ever heard of The Broken Record Technique? It's similar to a broken record. Come on… If you're an adult teacher reading this, you must be old enough to know what a broken record is and how it sounds when it's scratched and skipping. You know, a broken record just keeps repeating itself, right?

The Broken Record Technique works in our classrooms, and it's going to help us to get back to the real game of pedagogy—the art and science of teaching. Are you ready? Good. Here it goes. Hold on. The Broken Record technique consists merely of repeating yourself over and over again. Like a record that doesn't get mad or argue when it's skipping and repeating itself, neither are we getting mad or arguing when we're repeating ourselves.

For example, I say, "Hey, Shawn, can you open your book to page 10, please?" (Shawn doesn't want to open his book or do anything that day, so he tries to argue with me.)

Shawn says something like, "No, I don't want to open my book today because I'm tired."

I reply, "Alright. Shawn… Can you open your book to page 10, please?

He responds, "I'm not doing that. My mother kept me up all night, and Billy over here smells. Mister, tell Billy to stop bothering me with his stank!"

I state, "Okay. Shawn, open your book to page 10, please." Notice this time I'm not asking but instead directing him with The Broken Record Technique. I am ignoring the stench or at least the stench comment.

Shawn says, "These books suck."

"I hear you," I say with a smile on my face. "Now, Shawn, open your book to page 10, please."

You can see what's going on here. It's The Broken Record Technique. I say the same thing over and over and over without any real emotion, just like a broken record.

At that point, Shawn is probably thinking, "Damn. I hate that teacher sometimes." But, he opens his book to page 10 because he can't seem to engage his teacher in an argument. Not only that, his teacher isn't going away like some of the others who have tried before me.

You see, I refuse to let him suck me into the only option he only has available to him, which is to raise my blood pressure and engage in a power struggle through an argument. He is probably hoping that the argument ends with me walking away in disgust. He may be hoping that I kick him out of the classroom, which by the way, gives him exactly what he wants. By getting what he wants, he doesn't open his book and doesn't do the assignment.

Come on teachers… We all know this is true. He wants to get out of opening his book to page 10. He wants to look like he is in charge of what he is or isn't doing. Do you want to know something else too? The funny thing is that he really doesn't hate me, even if he did think it for a second or two, and perhaps mumbled it under his breath. By the way, I conveniently made sure that I didn't hear him saying those disrespectful things. Well, at least I acted like I didn't hear it.

I'm assuming that some of you reading this are probably saying, "Hey, I've done that before, and it worked." Do you know what would be even better though? It would be even better if we were all saying, "Hey, I did that today, and it worked." Present tense—not way back in the old days, but today. You see, we already know what to do to become more successful with difficult students because we have already been successful with difficult students many times in the past.

Where we run into problems with tough students is that we forget about our former successes with them. Another problem is that they get us so worked up that we cease to think straight. Any techniques that we might have to deal with these problematic kids effectively go right out the window thanks to our primitive fight or flight response when they successfully engage us in arguments.

If we could only get rid of that terribly old fight or flight response, then we'd be exceptionally better off as educators, wouldn't we? (Hey, wasn't that just another tie-down from Chapter 16?) The crazy thing about the primitive fight or flight response, which we all still have embedded deeply in our DNA, is that no matter how bad we want to partake in the flight or fight, we can't. We can't engage in flight because we have a job to do. Do not walk away from challenging students. It wouldn't be the adult thing to do by running away from our problems. Furthermore, we certainly can't fight… Well, you know why…Then, what are we to do?

I'll tell you what to do! The Broken Record Technique because it does work! We don't have to engage in fights or arguments with our students, and we don't have to take up the flight response and run away. In fact, we can stand our ground without any emotion and use The Broken Record Technique.

Some of you are probably wondering how long we should go on with The Broken Record Technique before we start looking like we're involved in some warped episode of an old Alfred Hitchcock movie, huh? Well, I'm going to tell you in the next chapter, okay? Another Tie-down, right?

*Chapter Twenty Three*

# The Death Stare

If you've done the preliminary relationship building, reverted to The Broken Record Technique, and asked the kid the same thing three, four, or five times, and it's still not working… If you feel like you're getting a little too close to making an accidental cameo in some crazy Alford Hitchcock Twilight Zone show somewhere in time, then stop asking that student to open his book to page 10 and give them The Death Stare!

"Da Da Da! Here comes The Death Stare."

The Death Stare works. I'm telling you, it works. I've used it a lot, and know for a fact that it does works. Here's the deal. A little spot right in-between their eyes becomes my target during my child-obliging Death Stare tactic. This little spot is the key to getting them to do what you want them to do. This targeted stare is like rubbing that magical little spot on your dog that gives you complete control of him. He kicks his leg in circles at a hundred miles an hour and always causes us to laugh. Yeah, come on you dog lovers. You know what I'm talking about… You know the spot.

Enough with the dirty dogs. Let's get back to the business of difficult students. When a student isn't successfully persuaded to dance to my song during The Broken Record Technique, then I abruptly stop for cause and effect. The kid is caught by surprise because he is trying to engage me in an argument. I won't say another word for a while. I stare at that little, magical spot between his eyes that I mentioned above.

The student is going to get slightly uncomfortable because he feels as if I'm staring into his soul through his eyes with my powerful stare. He gets the feeling that it is penetrating him. Some temperamental kids might think this is a staring competition. They may try to stare back at me, but they're not going to win this one. They are going to become uncomfortable first because they are trying to do what they think I am doing. However, what I'm not doing is staring into their eyes. They don't realize that I'm not staring into their eyes. This stare-down is an unfair competition that I'm going to win every time because I'm not looking into their eyes. Instead, I am staring at that magical "I-will-melt-and-behave" spot in between their eyes.

With The Death Stare Technique, we will keep our composure while they become increasingly uncomfortable challenging us. With this technique, we won't even feel like blinking. If we look right between their eyes, instead of into their eyes, we'll never even blink or feel any need whatsoever to blink or look away. We effortlessly can stand there looking at them all day long with our Death Stare. We won't feel any pressure at all. Conversely, they certainly will. It's almost like we quietly will them and melt them into behaving for us with our laser-beam stare.

This technique will help us look powerful to everyone witnessing it. It might even make us look taller than our students, and that's a good thing, especially for me since I'm short. On top of it all, the other students will see us standing our ground and think that we must be some bad-ass teacher. They may wonder whether or not we're part-time assassins. Perhaps, they shouldn't challenge us. Besides, we seem kind of nice to them with all those good things and Positive Postcards—why should they put themselves through that Death Stare with a nice-guy teacher?

My Death Stares have been so successful that I have had some of my toughest students melt in my presence as they have said, "No, Mister! Not the look. Don't do that. I hate it when you do that. Okay. I'll open my book to page 10."

I respond, "Thank you," and move on as long as they do open their book to page 10. The beautiful thing about the Death Stare is that it usually gets us out of giving other consequences, as well as arguing with our students.

Neither one is something that we, teachers, want to do anyway. It's a win, right? Tie-down!

Come on teachers. We all know it's true. Sometimes when we give a student a consequence, it's a consequence for us too, huh? I mean, do we really want to stay after school with this kid when we could be doing something else much more pleasant like cleaning our closet? Come on. There are better ways to use our time after school...

Hey, The Death Stare works! However, I don't use it that often. I don't have to use it that often because I have already created an excellent climate and have formed wonderful relationships with my students. Because of my established positive rapport, I almost never have to use The Death Stare. When I do use it in my classroom, the Death Stare doesn't damage the connections that I have with my students because of my invested time spent building relationships. An occasional Death Stare doesn't cause my students to think that I'm mean, unreasonable, and oppositional. Oh, by the way, we used to call that Op4 when I was in the Army.

In addition, The Death Stare works because it is primitive and speaks the primitive mind's language. Do you remember earlier in the book when I talked about the first brain, the emotional brain, the primitive brain, and how we all still have that brain inside our skulls buried under our neocortex? Well, that first brain still gives the orders when one is under stress. Students misbehaving coupled with The Death Stare will put them under pressure.

Furthermore, our students' first brains can't help but admire the strength and power they witness from watching us teachers stand our ground when we are applying the Death Stare onto some difficult student who needs to learn a lesson. The students may not be able to verbalize what is happening, or even rationalize it fully. Nevertheless, the dynamics are still there deep in the recesses of their minds somewhere captured in a picture format on how we held our ground. That deserves props. It's admirable. Don't worry. An occasional Death Stare won't damage your relationships with your students. Heck, it might even give them another reason to look up to you.

As I said before, I don't use the Death Stare that often. Consequently, when I do use it, it's effective. Do you want to know where I definitely get some good mileage out of The Death Stare? In the in-school suspension (ISS) room. Yeah, I use it in there sometimes. It makes those wanna-be tough guys… I mean wanna-be tough boys melt and shrivel under my superpowers. Well, they at least shield their eyes and pull back from their bad behavior, okay?

Here's a good question for you. What if you didn't engage in an argument and used The Broken Record Technique, and it didn't work? Following, you then used The Death Stare the way it was meant to be used and still had trouble getting your student to comply? Don't go anywhere because I'm going to tell you what to do about that in the next chapter.

*Chapter Twenty Four*

# Non-Emotional Consequences and Choices

The Broken Record Technique and the Death Stare help us in giving our students fewer consequences and makes it a little bit easier to maintain our positive relationships with our students, as well as the positive climate in our classrooms. However, occasions are still going to transpire when the Broken Record Technique and the Death Stare aren't enough, and a student is misbehaving again. Now what? Consequences are next.

The trick is to try to make the consequence that we're giving them feel more like a choice that they're making. You heard me right. We're going to use a psychological trick to ruse our students' little juvenile, primitive minds into thinking that we're still kind of okay because we didn't take away their superpowers by giving them a consequence. We're going to let them keep their superpowers because they can choose what they want instead of having a consequence from us. In their little youthful heads, they can justify (falsely) that they are still the ones in charge because they choose their consequence. Yeah... They'll think. Yeah... We'll think. It's a win-win, and we never tell them that it's a dual victory. They think they won. We know we won. We, teachers, would be happy to take these win-wins all day long, wouldn't we? Hey, that's another one of those tie-downs, isn't it? Oh, that's another, right?

Okay. Back to business. Here is how it works. This behavioral strategy isn't rocket science or even brain surgery. It's just a little psychology and a lot of dang-good teaching and classroom management. Here we go! Here's the scenario: Can you believe little Johnny still hasn't opened his book to page 10? After all, you've done for him… After all your efforts… You've bent over backward for him. Can't he see how much you care for him and how hard you're trying to help him? Doesn't he know that you've already cut him a bunch of breaks, and he owes you and owes you big time? I bet you can't believe that he still hasn't opened his book to page 10. It's heartbreaking, isn't it? I feel your pain, my fellow teacher.

Do you know what's even worse? Little Johnny is acting heartless! His meanness is starting to raise Cain in our fight-or-flight response. Part of us wants to shake little Johnny and make him understand how this is hurting him more than it is hurting us. Although, it doesn't feel like it sometimes, huh? Sometimes it feels like we're getting all the pain, and that's not fair, right?

The other part of our natural fight-or-flight response wants to flee—walk away and say, "If he can't see how foolish he is acting right now, then there is no hope for him. He doesn't deserve someone with hearts as big as ours, huh? We can do nothing more for him. We've done everything for him, and he doesn't even appreciate it. Dang him!"

We respond like this because we don't want to feel this way. We don't want to feel the pain he caused us anymore. We need to take a break from his crazy, disrespectful, and ungrateful behaviors and get away from him for a little bit, so we don't choke him. You see, we aren't cavemen or cavewomen anymore. The problem with our natural human inclinations and deep-seated DNA driven behaviors is that we can't shake him to make him understand and we can't walk away either. We can't act on our natural human responses, which makes us feel helpless and even hopeless. This situation depresses us and is not a good thing.

If we shake him, we lose our job and get arrested. Our arrest requires us to register as some crazy child abuser who will never be able to work again with youngsters because of these dang kids. If we walk away from little Johnny, then little Johnny gets his way again. Even worse, he just got rewarded instead of punished for acting crazy and disrespectful.

Now hold on. This scenario is about to get deeper. Are you ready? Good. Check out these primitive human emotions that we all have. If we do walk away, then little Johnny feels pleasure in us walking away because of his bad behavior. Instead of feeling pain or at least some discomfort for his bad behavior, which maybe he would have if we had stayed and given him a consequence, he now feels pleasure for misbehaving because we walked away.

Let me clarify this caveman stuff right now. Little Johnny's pain is something that he wants to stop immediately. When we do give him a consequence, he is going to say something like, "I don't care." He is somehow hoping this response to the stimuli (us) is going to help him to get rid of his pain (us walking away). The truth is that his callous response is full of faulty logic. His reaction won't work for him unless we willingly take on the burden of transferring his pain onto ourselves by falsely believing that he doesn't care and isn't in any pain.

After his callous response—"I don't care"—little Johnny is reading our faces hoping to see a sad facial expression that shows we just believed his little lie. He's hoping that now we're the ones who are in pain and will stop bothering him. Or… Maybe we'll scream at him and kick him out of the classroom because it's becoming too painful for us. We believed him and took on his pain, so he doesn't have to feel it. Us taking on the pain is okay also with little Johnny because he still gets what he wants—he doesn't have to deal with us anymore, nor does he have to open his book to page 10.

Little Johnny somehow knows that we just gave up our power in making him open up his book to page 10. He probably knows that it will probably be too painful for us in the future to ask him again to open up his book. Obviously, this time our efforts didn't work out so well for us, and we were the ones who wrongly ended up carrying the pain. Even more, if we forget and ask him again on another occasion to open his book, he'll do his best for a repeat to get us to carry his pain again. Why not? It worked last time for little Johnny, didn't it?

We all have heard of the basic pain-and-pleasure principle, right? We all tend to move toward pleasure and away from pain as fast as we can. We also have a good memory for what was painful and try not to repeat what caused us the pain in the future, like asking Little Johnny to open up his textbook. Another secret of this principle is that we will move faster to get away from pain than we will to move toward pleasure. Pain is a very effective deterrent. Does the big question now become who is going to carry and feel the pain? Little Johnny? Or us?

As long as our classrooms have these little Johnny's in them, and there are no signs of that stopping anytime soon, what are we, teachers, supposed to do? What is the remedy? Better yet, what is the trick to not even beginning the journey down those painful roads with our students? One of the many things we have to do is to get it into little Johnny's head that we are not going away. We're not going to lose our cool and harbor those feelings of pain that shouldn't be ours to carry. We are not going to walk away because of that pain, like many of little Johnny's teachers in the past have done. Additionally, we're going to accomplish this superhuman act through the strategy of Non-Emotional Consequences and Choices.

Let me tell you how non-emotional consequences work. First, hold your ground with your difficult students. While keeping a soft, calm, but confident voice, say something like, "Johnny, I need you to open your book to page 10. I'm not going to go away unless you open your book to page 10. If you want me to go away, then just choose to open your book to page 10. If you choose not to open your book to page 10, then you are choosing for me to stay right here, as well as choosing to stay for a lunch detention. It's your choice. You decide which one you want. Are you choosing for me to go away by opening to page 10, or are you choosing to have me stay right here, even through a lunch detention?"

If little Johnny chooses the lunch detention with his famous last words of, "I don't care," don't do what most teachers do at this point, which is to get mad, give the consequence, and then go away. That's what he wants. He wants you to go away. He is used to people getting so frustrated that they give up and go away. Heck, maybe he's even giving up on himself and wishes he could somehow go away from himself. Don't go away. Surprise him instead with something different.

Stay! Aren't there a whole bunch of songs about staying? Listen, you staying put is the last thing little Johnny is expecting right now. He thinks he's in the clear now, and you're going to go away all mad after giving him that dumb little detention that he's not going to serve anyway. Don't get angry. Simply stay put if the student plays the tough guy and says he's choosing the lunch detention. By selecting the lunch detention instead of opening his book, he also decided to have you hang out right by his side.

Sometimes, your continuing to stand there by his side will make little Johnny uncomfortable enough to open his book even though he chose the detention. Sometimes, his warped thinking is, "Well, I showed her. I picked the lunch detention instead. Now that I showed the whole class how tough I am and that I'm the boss, now I'll open my book only because I feel like it."

If staying put and not going away doesn't become uncomfortable enough for little Johnny to open up his book to page 10, then say something like, "Okay, now you get to make another choice. You can choose to open the book to page 10, and I'll go away, or you can choose to have your mom get a phone call on top of your lunch detention. Your choice. Which one do you want to choose?" If he chooses page 10, then walk away and hold him to that lunch detention, no matter what. If he decides the lunch detention and the phone call, make sure that you follow through with the lunch detention and phone call. Then, continue to stay put. Don't give him what he wants by walking away. Stay there and let him choose the next progressive consequence.

You have to make little Johnny feel like you're never going to walk away until he does what you tell him to do. Come up with a few more creative consequences, and follow through on them every time while giving him the option to make a choice. Allowing choice always allows you to say, "Hey, you chose this. All you have to do is to choose to open your book, and you can be choosing to have me walk away."

In the beginning, this may take more of your class time than you want to spend here. By doing this a few times, you're setting the example of how this class is going to run. Best of all, you're going to have a lot less stand-offish behavior because you once again thought ahead, thought differently about classroom management, and wisely invested your time on the front end to make the rest of the year go more smoothly.

What happens if this goes on and on and on, and you begin to feel like it's never going to end? That there is no real learning going on here? That you're wasting too much class time? Don't worry. Sit tight, and I'll tell you in the next chapter.

*Chapter Twenty Five*

# Assistance from Another Adult

I remember when I was in the Army. I completed infantry basic training at Fort Benning, Georgia in those old WWII barracks. It was during the sweltering heat of the summer of 1988 immediately after I graduated high school. During basic training, we had three drill sergeants assigned to each platoon, and I soon found out why the army assigns multiple authorities to each platoon. The army's model, notably, is the opposite of our country's education model of one teacher alone in a classroom full of kids.

In addition to having three platoon drill sergeants, several more are standing and waiting on the peripheral. While they may be involved with other platoons or in general overall, supervisory roles, they are more than happy to jump in and assist at a moment's notice. Drill sergeants' eyes are everywhere watching the new candidates sweat it out. The Army drill sergeants can gang up on the recruits when one of them screws up. On the contrary, the education world has the opposite model that encourages the students to gang up on the lone teacher in the classroom. It's typical for classes to be bursting at the seams with students overflowing every nook and cranny of the room, and usually, the teacher doesn't have any help. More often than not, any complaint about the situation is frowned upon by the school administration.

Anytime, and every time (some psychology here again), a soldier screwed up in basic training, two drill sergeants jump in his face and 'smoked' him, as they used to say in the Army. The third drill sergeant looks for anyone else who is off task, laughing or even smiling. This third drill sergeant puts any other undisciplined soldiers in the front-leaning rest—push-up position. Those soldiers must have forgotten where they were when they cracked a smile. These weak and undisciplined privates will remain in the front-leaning rest until the one drill sergeant gets tired of looking at their shaking arms. Meanwhile, the other two drill sergeants continue to smoke that poor candidate who stepped out of line first. When other soldiers witness this, no one wants to be the first to step out of line anymore and chance being hauled over the coals.

Regardless of where they come from, it doesn't take long for these young recruits to shape up and act like they're in the Army, and not back on the block with their boys, or girlfriends. With that Army model in mind, I want to tell you now that this approach is not the kind of assistance I will be referring to in this chapter when I talk about the strategy of Assistance From Another Adult…

If we want, we, teachers, can take a moment here to amuse ourselves a little bit by daydreaming about what this method of Army assistance would be like in our classrooms for just a few moments before we read the rest of this chapter… I won't tell anyone… I promise… Nor will I think less of you for entertaining these military-style educational thoughts.

Now that we're done with that, here's the real deal in the real world of public education. Now and then, it makes sense to get a little help with our difficult students. I call this strategy Assistance From Another Adult. If you find the Non-Emotional Consequences and Choosing strategy going nowhere, at some point, you're going to have to change gears. Otherwise, you're going to waste too much class time involved in a power struggle with your difficult student(s). As mentioned earlier, make him feel the pain by staying put, but also be wise enough to know when to move on. These are the tough times where it helps a teacher to have another adult in the room, or at least one available somewhere to assist you.

Ready for some more psychology here? Okay, here it is. Something as simple as the other adult being the opposite sex or gender than you helps. If you're a male, you may be dealing with a kid that can't stand his dad, and he dislikes men in general. Maybe you look like his dad. A female adult may be precisely what the doctor ordered. This student may comply with the female adult and open his book to page 10. He may feel that he won because he didn't do it for you, the man who reminds him of his deadbeat father. He did it for her, the one who reminds him of his angel-like mom. Hey, it's not perfect, but we'll take it.

Sometimes, your students may even verbalize this preference by saying something like, "I ain't doing it for you. I'm doing it for Ms. XYZ." He'll act as if he won. But, to tell you the truth, you both won. You won because he finally opened his book to page 10, and that's what you wanted all along. He won because he opened his book to page 10, feels victorious or unbeaten, and has a possible chance at getting some amount of education.

The reverse scenario using opposite gender dynamics also works. If you're a female teacher, maybe a male adult can get this kid to do what you're asking him to do without all the hassle you're getting from him. In the end, it's a win-win. If the opposite sex isn't available, maybe just a different voice will do the trick… Don't be too proud. Recruit the help of an adult that is in the vicinity. If that doesn't work, then maybe a different voice of a school administrator will work the magic.

Sometimes nothing is working, and nothing is going to work on that particular day. During those times, it might make sense to give the kid a break from the classroom environment by having someone take a walk with him, sitting him briefly in another class, guidance office, social worker's area, or in-school suspension room. You might even send him home for the day. Going home might be what he needs at that moment if nothing else is working.

Listen, I get it, and I know we don't want to send kids home very often. Yet, every once in a while, maybe the youngster genuinely can't hold it together anymore that day and needs a break of some sort… Hey, similar to what Collin Powell always said during the Vietnam War, "Things will look better in the morning."

Use the other adult and the different adult voice, especially the opposite gender voice whenever you can to maintain the relationships and positive climate in the classroom. This dynamic will help you avoid power-struggles and additional consequences which we really don't want. If it doesn't work and the kid does escalate it to the point where he needs to go home, what should we do then?

Sit tight, and I'll tell you in the next chapter.

*Chapter Twenty Six*

# Call Them At Home

Another thing we, teachers, can do to build those favorable relationships once a kid has been sent home by an administrator is to... Are you ready for this? Okay...Here it comes... Call them at home when everything has cooled off.

I know you may not have cooled off all the way from what you perceive as extremely disrespectful behavior. I know you may still be a little mad at the kid. Perhaps the last thing you may want is more of that kid. You may not want to talk to that kid again so soon. Nevertheless, you should!

Listen! I know you had a hard day with that kid. Believe it or not, picking up that 800-pound phone sitting securely on your desk and calling that troubled kid at home is a good idea. It is worth the effort. I know you can do this. I know you can be enough of an adult to push aside your feelings and do the adult thing by making that call.

Go ahead. Just do it. When you make that telephone call, say something like, "Hey, Johnny. Yeah, um... Listen, I know you had a rough day today and got suspended... and all that. But, hey look, I just want to make sure that you're... umm, okay. Okay? Are you okay, buddy? Everything alright, man? Listen, I'm only asking because you know I love you, right? I love you like you were one of my own children, and I want you back here tomorrow, buddy. You come back here tomorrow, and you and I are going to have a good time. Okay, pal? Hey, tomorrow is a new day, and you're going to get your work done, alright? We're going to have a good time tomorrow and learn a whole bunch of stuff too. Okay, kiddo?"

At this point, it's refreshing to hear that kid, quiet and at a loss for words. It might be the first time you've ever heard that kid quiet and lost for words, and that's okay. That's a good thing. As a matter of fact, it's an exceptionally good thing. It means you caught him by surprise, and he's thinking about you. Hopefully, he's also thinking about what he did to get sent home. That's a good thing too. Do you know what else a good thing is? It's a good thing that he doesn't have to put on a show at that moment for his friends who aren't there watching him. It's just him and you on the phone. He's different when it's only him and you, without all the other distractions.

The thing is that we didn't do it. We didn't do anything to this student. He did it all to himself. He shouldn't be mad at us because he is the one who caused his problems. Deep down inside he knows that. Don't reinforce the little lie that he is telling himself right before we called which is that he is in trouble because his teacher doesn't like him. Maybe the untruth is that his teacher is a jerk.

You extinguish that lie by calling his home and telling him that you can't wait to have him back in your class tomorrow because you are going to have a good time. You say to him, "We are going to do our work, learn some cool stuff." You say, "You and me, we are going to start figuring it all out, and we're going to have a good time."

These types of things begin to sink into that little skull of his and weaken that lie he's telling himself about you disliking him. This strategy will help both of you to get over that unimportant argument and begin to like each other again. Try it sometime. Call their homes. Shock them into liking you and behaving better for you!

*Chapter Twenty Seven*

# Don't Take It Personal

I know this is easier said than done. It's hard not to take it personally when we are human beings. When someone says mean, nasty things to us, it hits home. It hurts. Sometimes we can't help but feel angry, or can we?

We are the adults. Our minds are more developed than our teenage students'. They may not know this yet, but we are way cooler than they think. Hey, it's not their fault that they don't know this. They don't have the ability at their tender age to think as we can think.

Their prefrontal cortexes (PFCs) are still developing and will continue to grow for many more years. Their ability to think about what's cool or not cool often takes the amygdala shorter and quicker route of thinking. Their brains' shortcuts were created by the primitive first brain that we talked about earlier, and these shortcuts are short-changing them. This part of the mind says, "Hey, you don't have time to think right now about that sabre-tooth tiger. Just run!"

The beautiful thing is that, as adults, our prefrontal cortexes (PFCs) are more developed than our youths' PFCs! Hooray! As I said, we really can't blame kids for not being able to think like us. Nor can we blame them for not thinking that we are cool. Yup. We're way cooler than they initially thought. Again, the reason is that their young minds are limited; not like ours though… Our thoughts are unlimited because we are the adults with all the superpowers… Those little kids have none… "None!" I said…

Our students don't know yet that thoughts become things. That's right. Thoughts do eventually become things. We adults recognize this to be true because our life experiences have shown us that what we persistently think about usually comes true. Conversely, the kids who are still in their developmental stage don't realize that thoughts become things. They can't and won't know that thoughts become things because they are too young to understand it as we do. What does this have to do with anything? Read on. The explanation is coming in the next paragraph.

Here's the thing. Insults do hurt. They sting. When our students are difficult, it hurts us at least a bit. But, as I said earlier, thoughts become things. We, adults, know that the things we think about tend to materialize in our lives. The things we contemplate most become the little story that we tell ourselves over and over again. The stories that we tell ourselves repeatedly eventually become the way we perceive reality. These thoughts become our reality. Will it be a good reality or a painful reality?

We cool and smart adults know our thoughts and perceptions become our realities. The young ones who are sitting in front of us in our classrooms are still trying to develop. They're still trying to be more like us, and they don't even realize that they're trying to become more like us. Well… They can't be like us—at least not right now. They have to wait their turn. They have to wait until they're all grown up and have kids of their own who give them a hard time before they hear their voices sounding like ours.

We, adults, recognize that we create our reality through the things we think and tell ourselves. If we take our students' unsubstantiated insults and slurs about our character personally, as a new true narrative, we comprehend that we will increase the stress in our lives. We know that stress can be a bad thing that has the capability of making us very sick. Being as cool as we, adults, are and as smart and mature as we are with our kick-butt PFCs, we know we're not going to let some runny-nose kid with adolescent acne stress us out and make us sick.

***We are not going to take it personally!*** Nor are we going to regress and think more like them or act more like them. Our nose is not going to run, nor are we going to grow pimples. We are not going to believe their insults or take them personally because we know thoughts become things. We're going to train our brain to think about only good stuff, so those good thoughts will eventually become good things for us in the future.

However, even with all this great advice, each and every one of us still knows that not taking it personally is easier said than done. Be that as it may, since we possess secret adult superpowers called metacognition, we can, if truth be told, think about our thinking. Kids don't have this ability. We aren't going to take our students' insults or poor behavior personally because we know better. As I said before, nor are we going to let someone else stress us out and make us sick. Believe it or not, we know that not personalizing things is better for us. Moreover, we know that it's better for the classroom climate, relationships, and kids. We mustn't take it personally!

Come on, teachers! We remember the old song that we used to sing, right? (Tie down) "I'm rubber, and you're glue. Whatever you say to me, bounces off me and sticks to you." We've been practicing this rubber-glue-not-taking-it personal thing way longer than our students have. We got them here. Heck, we're so cool and advanced that we even sing songs about it.

I'm going to go out on a limb here and say that we totally cool adults have sung majestically about this rubber-glue-not-taking-it personal thing. I'm sure some of us have belted off some excellent tunes in our parents' cars as kids. I bet some of us still do it in our cars after a hard day of teaching as we're white-knuckling the steering wheel and trying to decide if we still want to go to the gym to pound the heck out of the weights. We might be trying to decide whether or not we want to go to the local tavern to pound something else... Do what I did and go to the gym to pound the heck out of those weights while practicing not taking it personally. Trust me. It's the much, much wiser choice.

Seriously, all joking aside, folks. Taking our students' painful comments and unacceptable behavior personally does no one any good. Not making it personal is the only high road. It's the best possible choice all around. Not taking it personally is a choice. Choose wisely.

# PART 6

## THE SECOND ADULT

## ELECTRONICS

## Q & A

*Chapter Twenty Eight*

# The Second Adult

Some of the present-day classrooms in our public schools are staffed with more than one adult, especially if they are inclusion classrooms. Being an inclusion class, it will have a regular education classroom teacher who typically is the content expert and, for the most part, leads the classroom. The second adult is a special education teacher who is the pedagogy expert and primarily spends time helping a few of the kids in need of additional support. The special education teacher also floats around the classroom and helps other kids as well.

Public school classrooms may also have a para-educator, a student-teacher, or an intern from a local college. Having extra adult educators in any classroom is awesome. In contrast, you want to know what's not awesome? Territorialism. Many teachers are territorial and don't love the idea of others intruding into their classes and their space.

Whether knowingly or unknowingly, many mainstream teachers do not effectively use the second adult assigned to their rooms nor do they fully appreciate this valuable resource. This situation is sad because they have been blessed to have a second adult in the classroom. All too often, many of these second adults feel the tension of their intrusion. They don't know what to do about it or how to best use their abilities to help the students, let alone the other teacher.

What should the second adult in the classroom do? First and foremost, they should build a positive relationship with the other educator. Developing this relationship will help classroom teachers push their fear or anxiety aside and figure out a way to best work as a team of educators to improve the students' lives, abilities, and performances.

You know... I can still remember when I was in the United States Army Basic Training, and we had a head-drill sergeant and two assistant drill sergeants assigned to our platoon. The three drill sergeants worked as a fine-tuned machine. They worked as a model of a perfect team. Each drill sergeant had full authority and approval from command to dish out push-ups and anything else they deemed appropriate for the moment.

These drill sergeants did a great job. The three of them took fifty, individual young men who came from all over the U.S. and a wide variety of demographics, cultures, socio-economic classes, religions, ages, and whatever else and molded us all into a finely tuned machine. We thought alike, fought alike, and shared one heartbeat.

Education could learn something from this military model. Teachers don't always know how best to carry out this teamwork thing. Rarely are educators given common-planning time to help them figure it out together. Many times educators are on their own—just winging it—and can only hope for the best once multiple adults step into the classroom.

During these ambiguous times when there is a second adult in the classroom, the special education teacher, or the para, or whoever it is, needs to help develop the teamwork. This second adult can start by acting like he or she is there for all students.

Additionally, the second adult in the classroom needs to stand up and walk around the room more than merely sit and listen to the teacher explaining directions or presenting a lesson. The psychological effect of an adult sitting down puts that adult on the same level as the kids. They are sitting there passively listening while the lead teacher is standing, walking around the room, and towering over everyone... including the second adult.

Being taller, bigger, than the students who are sitting down, smaller, at their desks holds some hidden psychology. The standing teacher has the position of power, and this standing-tall strategy needs to be used by all the adult educators who are in the classroom. Teachers, no matter what their role, should not be on the same level as the students.

The second adult in the classroom, while upon his or her feet, needs to participate in the lesson as often as possible. If he or she isn't familiar with the content, then they should ask the classroom teacher a bunch of questions. Verbal volleying going back and forth between the adult educators creates a back-and-forth exchange which makes the class more interactive and more fun.

Also, because there is more action going on in class, students pay better attention and become more engaged. If the lead classroom teachers complain that they are being slowed down, then they need to be told respectfully that the questions asked are the ones that the students are too afraid to ask. And…this creates a win-win for everyone!

A few other things that both adult educators need to do in the classroom are to collaborate, compromise, and trust. Classes configured with extra support are precisely what many of our students need to perform better. Good communication between the adult educators is an absolute must if they are going to collaborate effectively and achieve this goal. Since common-planning time is rare, the adult educators are going to have to go out of their way to create some time to talk, plan, and evaluate how they are doing. This teamwork won't always be easy, but it is a must if the inclusion or extra-support strategy is going to be successful.

Life is full of compromises because it deals with people. Well, guess what? Inclusion teaching or multiple adults in a classroom also is full of compromises. Every adult has something valuable to offer, and we need to tap those sources of excellence, so the best results possible in the teaching and learning process are achieved. Realistically, no one ever gets everything they want, but if we all get some of what we want, it's a win-win-win. The classroom teacher wins. The second adult in the classroom wins, and so do the students!

Finally, I want to add that we, adult educators, have to trust each other. Any organization that is lacking trust never entirely succeeds. Since we're talking about educating our next generation, we all need to succeed wildly.

Spending some extra time together for better collaboration added to the give-and-take of compromise mentioned above is a good start for building trust. Trust never stops. We all need to work on it continuously. When done with fidelity, the schools and classrooms become authentic learning institutions. Even more, special education teachers and paras viewed as positions that are inferior to the classroom teacher will become a thing of the past.

*Chapter Twenty Nine*

# Electronics

Hmm… Electronics is a tough one. Because technology is innovative by nature, it always seems to be one step ahead of the laws of the land and the rules of the schools. To be honest with you, I think I can compare electronics to that old tube of toothpaste again that was mentioned earlier in the book. This generation of students has already squeezed electronics out of the tube, and putting them back is not a feasible possibility. This tube of electronics even has its own social media channel now called, YouTube!

Our kids have grown up with electronics. They don't know anything different, even though we, adults, do know something different. As I just said, I believe that electronics are out of the tube, and no way exists to get it back inside that tube. Oh, we can try, but, we are going to make a big old mess and get frustrated. In the end, we're not going to accomplish anything anyway.

We have to think differently about electronics. Our old way of thinking about these new devices is a losing battle. One should know by now that I don't promote power-struggles between the students and staff. Let's look for a win-win, instead. Electronics is a battle that we don't have to fight and shouldn't be fighting. Let's find a productive way to use it because this unnecessary fighting is making it harder for us to build relationships with our students. It's also making it tougher for us to maintain the relationships that we already have.

A better way to infuse our students' world (an electronic world) into our world of education does exist. The two worlds should be able to come together as one where there is a great deal of good teaching and learning, as well as fun, going on for our kids. After all, isn't it true that public education exists for our kids? Public education wasn't created for the adults, right? It was created for the kids, right? Let's teach them in a fun way that fits into their world and the way they want to learn.

I believe that we can come up with some good ideas if we all put our heads together and include as many students as possible in the decision-making process of using electronics in school. Many schools have their own Bring Your Own Device (BYOD) policies. Let's learn more about them and find out what's working and what's not working. Let's use the best of what others are doing to build digital citizenship for our students in a responsible manner. Let's steal their ideas that seem to be working. That sounds like fun, doesn't it?

Hey, it might make sense for kids to be able to use electronics in the hallway and cafeteria and maybe when they're doing solo work in a study hall or something like that. Maybe use them during independent seat work, for instance during the last ten or fifteen minutes of class when they are quietly working at their seat. This time would be an excellent opportunity for them to chill with their work and music. Maybe we can even use this time as a naturally built-in reward for them doing an excellent job during the other thirty minutes of class.

Today's kids multitask like crazy. Heck, we even multitask like crazy. Okay, I hear you. We, adults, multitask just short of craziness. But, think about this—how many times have we been in a meeting and received a text from our spouses and discreetly zipped something back to them about picking up one of the kids from practice? That quick text didn't mean that we were not paying attention at our professional meeting. We were just multitasking.

Think about this. Our students are even better at multitasking then we are. We need to think differently when it comes to electronics. The world has changed. We must somehow change and stop creating power-struggles with our students that we don't have to create.

Students having some time to use their electronics is an excellent leverage point for teachers to use in getting kids to put away their electronics when we don't want them out. Having part of our classes academically involving electronics somehow is also another good idea. Finally, using humor, instead of anger to get a kid to put away their electronics, is always the better road to take.

If you have to take the phone away from one of your students because school policy is forcing you to do it, then consider an experiment performed by the authors Adam Galinsky and Maurice Schweitzer of the book, Friend & Foe. When their research assistants went up to strangers and said that they needed to use their phone because they had a very important phone call to make, most people didn't trust them. Only nine percent gave up their phone. However, when the researchers did the same thing, but first apologized for the rainy day, forty-three percent of those strangers gave up their phone. That's a 400% increase in the number of strangers that gave up their phones.

If you're forced to take a kid's phone, then apologize for something first. Interestingly, it almost seems like it doesn't even matter what you apologize for at the moment. Even apologizing for the weather seems to warm people up to you more and makes them trust you more. It helps to make them want to give you their phone. If complete strangers give up their phone, then I think we should have some success with students who we know by using this strategy of apologizing for something first.

If there is something vital going on that you need to have 100% attention and there is no wiggle room for any electronic diversions, put the students in a circle where everyone is looking at each other. No one can conceal what they are doing. This inability to hide is an example of what the International Institute for Restorative Practices does with restorative circles. You can learn from and use this method effectively in your classroom. Learn more at https://www.iirp.edu/index.php?option=com_rsform&view=rsform&formId=7&Itemid=123

If your school has a zero tolerance for electronics, then get ready for some power-struggles between teachers and students. Also, be prepared for some strained relationships. If a school is going to go down this road, then I believe the school administration needs to take the lead on this.

They need to invest in the pouch-policy program where the administration has stations set up at the entrance of the school. Each kid's electronics goes into a sealed pouch, and then that pouch goes into the kid's pocket, not to be opened until administration opens them again as the kids are exiting the school.

Finally, on another note, I frequently hear how electronics are changing our kids' brains. I often hear how electronics are bad and are going to ruin our youths' brains. I'm not fully convinced that any new learning tool, like electronics, is going to ruin our kids' brains. After all, didn't they say the same thing about writing at its genesis? They said that if people could write down details, we wouldn't have to remember anything anymore and that would cause us to lose our ability to story tell. They said that writing would cause our brains to atrophy. I don't think that has happened. Do you? Hmm… Not so sure the electronics one will happen either…

*Chapter Thirty*

# Q & A

**A REAL TEACHER'S QUESTION:** When I went to school, I didn't want to draw attention to myself. I wanted the teachers to love me. I wanted to be my teachers' favorite student. Kids today, don't care about this anymore. They don't care if their teachers correct them, and they are not at all embarrassed in front of their peers. I am still trying to figure out why or what dynamic has changed. Do you have any ideas of what has happened?

**DANIEL BLANCHARD'S RESPONSE:** Reality TV is partially responsible. I think the low-costs paychecks the television networks are giving to the majority of those wannabee stars is indirectly hurting our society, especially our youth.

They are not real actors. They are not real professionals who have worked hard to break into show business. These are low-quality people. Sadly, none of them are the least bit embarrassed about the dumb things they do on these television shows. It's all about the ratings and their five minutes of fame. They don't care about anything because they can act like complete jerks and make a lot of money doing it.

Most of these reality television people are nothing more than new-era Jerry Springer guests. Most of them have no skills. Most aren't even likable. Yet, they are still rewarded with riches and fame (something all our students want).

Why are we paying them to act like losers? What do they really do? What contribution do they make? None. That's the answer! Nothing! Absolutely nothing! Nonetheless, they are a hundred times more popular than our kids' teachers and much, much richer than our kids' teachers. Unfortunately, our youths are quicker to look up to rich, famous people as role models than their teachers simply because these crazy people are on television and all over social media. Furthermore, as stated earlier, our teens' brains aren't developed enough at this point in time to know better. Someday they will, but not today.

Reality TV is hurting our society and our youth. Remember, our youths are the next generation of leaders who will eventually be the ones in charge and taking care of us. Reality TV needs to take some responsibility for what they're doing. But, they won't. Making a buck is more important to them than our youth and the future of our country.

Do you want to know who else needs to take some responsibility? Some of them include professional athletes, music stars, movie stars, YouTube sensations, and anyone else who has our youths' eyeballs on them. Teachers can't do it all by themselves. Nor can parents. It's supposed to take a village to raise a child. However, we have way too many people in that village who have our youths' eyeballs on them saying dumb things like, "I'm not a role model. I never asked to be a role model. Don't make me your role model."

Wrong answer, Dude! As soon as you did something to put our highly impressionable youths' eyeballs on you, you became a role model. Like it or not! Step up and be the big star that you're trying to tell everyone that you are. Do the right thing and help our kids succeed in a positive way that makes a positive difference in this world! Be responsible. After all, responsible turned around is the ability to respond. Plus, you have that ability, superstar, right? Well, you keep telling the whole world about your skills, so why don't you put your money where your mouth is and show some ability in being responsible to our youth…?

Now the big question becomes, what can teachers do? Well, I say let's break down the walls that kids have put up between us. Let's pull them away from the phony Reality Star of the week who doesn't seem ever to be embarrassed by his inappropriate behavior. Let's pull the kids aside as often as we can to teach them right and wrong. Let's spend a lot of extra time with kids. Let's try to help kids any way we can. Let them know that they're not supposed to act like Reality TV stars. Let them know that none of it is real and none of it can last. These phony Reality Stars' fake five minutes of fame is going to end in a fiery crash. Finally, always model appropriate behavior, teachers, and point out what kids are doing wrong in a way that doesn't embarrass them.

**A REAL TEACHER'S QUESTION:** Do kids even understand what's going on? Kids watch these trendy shows like Sponge Bob that have this sophisticated sense of humor which kids are probably not even aware. Then, kids emulate or at least try to mimic their favorite characters' bad behaviors. It's just part of their make up now, isn't it? Is there anything we can do about it?

**DANIEL BLANCHARD'S RESPONSE:** I agree with you. The cartoons today are full of that sophisticated humor which in many instances is nothing more than a whole bunch of sarcasm. It drives me crazy when I hear sarcasm coming from a cartoon. I wonder what the heck has happened to our world. Our kids are supposed to be able to watch cartoons. Cartoons and other kid shows are supposed to be safe. They aren't. Cartoons are teaching our kids bad things like sarcasm, rudeness, terrible manners, and outright inappropriate behaviors. It's making me mad as hell!

In my mind, it doesn't even matter if kids understand the inappropriate sophisticated humor or not. The humor being sophisticated is an obvious cop out by the media so they can make another buck while saying that kids don't understand it. Sadly, crap and other terrible things like that sell. The fact that the humor is sophisticated is a cover plan for the people making money.

Sorry to say, many parents are overwhelmed. Thus, many aren't making the extra effort to help their kids watch better media than this garbage we're seeing on television these days. Kids don't have to know that something is inappropriate, rude, and outright wrong to repeat it. They also don't have to fully comprehend that it's dangerous to copy it and try it. Regrettably, kids are copying their favorite characters from television and social media, even though they are clueless that many of their favorite characters are losers not worthy of imitation. Perhaps kids should emulate someone who is behaving appropriately, who is kind, and who is trying to make this world a better place—like their teachers or coaches...

Here's that big question again. What can we, teachers, do? Well, let's begin with continuing to be the great people that we are. Teachers are the real deal! It's true! Next, let's try to be a little more interesting when we're around kids, even if that means putting on five shows a day in class. Also, let's allow the kids to see us a little more often outside of our teacher role so that they know we have a life beyond teaching. Let them see us and hang out with us outside of the classroom. Let them find out that we are good people, good role models, and good citizens. Teach them that we are the ones they should be copying!

**A REAL TEACHER'S QUESTION:** One of the things that my district is doing is to have teachers give at least four positive praises to every one negative comment they make to students. For some people, that's hard because they're trying to keep their students on task and at the same time they're looking around for more positive things to say to their students. I'm a little worried about the authenticity of this 4:1 system. What do you think?

**DANIEL BLANCHARD'S RESPONSE:** Well, I agree that more praise than negative comments is always a good idea. Being more positive does help improve the climate in the class and can help students know that their teachers do care about them. However, a system is still just a system. It's not human. It's a system. Any system has its flaws, regardless of how well-intended its creator. I'm not saying that a system can't be good. Systems can be good. Some are very good. The question is whether you want to be a good teacher or a great teacher? Systems can help make you a good teacher. However, only your humanity can make you a great teacher. Let me ask you again. Do you want to be a good teacher or a great teacher?

If you want to be a great teacher, then you're going to have to be cognizant that within a system you might be losing out on chances of human contact because you're too busy calculating your numbers instead of interacting with humans. You're losing time with your students that you'll never get back because you're preoccupied with the 4:1 ratio, instead of your students. Also, when we strictly act within the system, our students will eventually figure out that it's a system, and they will feel like it's not authentic praise that you're giving them. It's only something you're being paid to do.

What should teachers do? Well, let's begin by putting a human touch on everything you do in your classrooms, even if you're forced to operate within a system. Err on the side of thinking more about the kids than the numbers. If you do this, your numbers will be okay or pretty dang close anyway.

Administrators, if you are reading this, please realize that if someone is in the teaching business or the business of school administration, then that person is really in the people business. People come first with systems and numbers second. Teachers, if your school administrators don't realize this yet, then it's your job, as the classroom teacher, to advocate for your students and yourself. Conduct yourselves as if you're in the people business. Remember, you are! Gently, but often, remind your school administrators to the fact that education is a people business. The great Einstein said that the intellect has no personality and thus could only serve, not lead. Don't let number crunching lead all your classroom efforts.

**A REAL TEACHER'S QUESTION:** Dan, where did you learn all this stuff? Did you learn it from some behavioral program that you took? What resources did you look at that we can look at too?

**DANIEL BLANCHARD'S RESPONSE:** That's a good question. I'm glad you brought that up. Most of the stuff that I'm talking about in this book, I came up with on my own. I worked out many of the bugs by practicing these things over the last two decades as both a special education teacher and mainstream, regular education teacher in Connecticut's largest inner-city high school. I've seen a lot over the years, and maybe some of the best advice I can give you is that you have to get to know your students. Don't wait! You have to quickly learn what's going to work for a particular group of students in front of you. Know who is sitting in front of you. Know what the strengths and weaknesses of your students are academically, socially, and emotionally. Never be afraid to steal. Steal resources and good teaching ideas whenever you can. Go ahead and steal anything you want out of this book that fits your personality and makes sense to you and your teaching style. Feel free to tweak anything in this book to meet the unique needs of your class. This book is not a manual that needs to be followed precisely, but rather a way to think differently about educating difficult students.

As for more resources, I have a section near the end of this book that will help you with that as well.

# PART SEVEN

## CONCLUSION

*Chapter Thirty One*

# Conclusion

In closing, let me say I don't always reach every single kid. I'm not always successful with every single student. Many kids have been in my classes over the years that I have looked at and thought, "Geez I'm trying so hard to win this kid over, but does this kid ever take a break from acting like a _ _ _? Holy cow! Imagine what that kid must be like at home?"

Except, the funny thing, or maybe I should say an ironic thing, is that a lot of those troubled and difficult kids come back and visit me later. They might visit me the following year when they are in a different grade and have a different teacher. They might come by to see me in the hallway during passing time when they stop to talk. Sometimes, I hear them say to another student as they're walking by, "Hey, that's Mr. Blanchard. He's the best teacher I ever had, Man." I think, "Boy, I thought that kid hated me. I guess once again that I was wrong." I have been wrong a lot in my life.

Sometimes, it takes until they graduate for this special moment to happen. Many times they come back three or four years later. I've had former students years later who have walked right into my classroom out of nowhere while I was teaching. They announced to the class, "This is Mr. Blanchard. You all better listen to what he is saying because this guy knows what he is talking about. He is the best teacher I ever had." I'm like, "Dang! This job really can be awesome, sometimes…"

Honestly, I'm still waiting for a few of my former students to come back. I still have my mind's eye and my big ol' heart on a few of them who still haven't come back yet. That's just the reality of the job we have. It's hard, it's exhausting, and it's difficult and very frustrating. If we are going to survive, we have to begin the process of becoming that person who is a quality person and who is also having some fun teaching while building that positive classroom climate and those positive relationships with our students. Someday, those extremely tough ones do come back and thank us for changing their lives.

Our former students returning for a visit is the sort of thing that also makes teaching more enjoyable. These rewards will help our health and our longevity (Hopefully, you get a longevity bonus).

Finally, you've probably heard that old motto that teachers aren't supposed to smile until Christmas. Well, I have some news for you. That teaching strategy no longer works. Throw out that old motto and start a new slogan of doing nothing but smiling until Christmas. Trust me, you'll be way better off, and your class will be way better off because they'll be continuously wondering what the heck you're up to now…

*Chapter Thirty Two*

# Expert Tips

## TIPS FROM EXPERTS ON WORKING WITH DIFFICULT CHILDREN

*Carole Clifford—Former Teacher and American Federation of Teachers Professional Development Director:*

"Greeting each student every day at the door with a personal hello. For example, you look great today. I really like that shirt...let's shake hands...can't wait to see you shine today...Also, be consistent every day. Many students came back and said, 'I could depend on you to be the same every day, and you made me feel safe.' Lastly, treat each day as brand new. Nothing that happened the day before carried over be it a discipline matter or other. Start the day off brand new."

*Oscar Cielos Staton—Teacher and Educational Consultant:*

"As educators, we don't get the necessary background knowledge on each of our students. We don't have the necessary information on challenges as well as passions outside of the school environment. Students we label difficult didn't just happen overnight. There is likely a path on which an institution and/or individual failed them previously." That being said, these students require structure. There should be rules, rewards, and consequences in place so they may be successful. These should be applied consistently to all students. There should be many opportunities in place for small moments of success. They need to know they are cared for. For trust to exist, these need to be in place."

*Larry Fenn—School Superintendent:*

"One size does not fit all, but behavior management requires serious diagnoses of students unique characteristics and a prescriptive plan which when implemented needs careful monitoring by all stakeholders—parents, teachers, administrators and of course counselors and the student."

*Dr. Allen N. Mendler—Educator, school psychologist, and author:*

"Discipline that lasts relies on teaching better behavior and emphasizes relationship, respect, and responsibility rather than detention, suspension, and trips to the office. It is about making school a welcoming place for all students, including the difficult ones, and being relentless in refusing to give up even when students make themselves hard to like."

*Julia G. Thompson—Retired Teacher and Best-Selling Author:*

"Focus on building confidence in your difficult students who are so used to failing at school. When you instill self-belief in your students, they can transform into lifelong learners, regardless of their age or ability level. You have given them a reason to try—to not shut down. Students who are confident in their ability to succeed will also find it easy to feel positive about the class and about their relationship with you. Use every tool that you can think of to convince your students that you enjoy being with them and that you find them capable of success. Turning around a negative self-image takes time, patience, and effort, but it can make all the difference in the world for your students."

*Jamie Edward Ciofalo—School Administrator, Author, Speaker, and Educational Consultant:*

"As a school administrator, I advise those who work with students experiencing academic or behavioral difficulties that it is not the student who is difficult—it is the student's circumstances that are difficult, so be sure to teach with tough skin and a tender heart."

*Dr. Thomas Reale—Former Indiana School Superintendent:*

"I've found that working with difficult kids involves building personal relationships by getting to know them as individuals who have their own lives, interests, and value systems. Critical in trying to relate to and motivate them is to avoid assuming that what motivates you motivates them. Their life experience is very unlikely to be yours. Keep that in mind if you want to meet them where they actually are rather than where you think they should be."

*Phillip Jarvis—President of Transitions Canada Coalition, a not-for-profit national coalition of education, business, government, and civic leaders:*

"Students can be difficult because their brains have suffered in powerful and enduring ways due to environmental conditions at home or school like stress, anger, fear, humiliation, poverty, neglect, or shame. As challenging as it can be, teachers who truly want to reach these students must show them love, acceptance, and patience while trying to find those things about which they care passionately and which light them up. Like all adolescents, difficult students need to know that when they discover their purpose, they can tap incredible potential within, master more than they can imagine, and truly make a difference in the world."

*Connie Bombaci—Retired Teacher, Associate Principal, and Award-winning Author:*

"Keeping students' needs as the top priority is key in working with any behavior. Their circumstances are paramount in planning, making decisions, and approaching difficult situations. In the long run, our kids want to be accepted, cared about, and understood. Add forgiveness and kids 'climb mountains' for us. They need, sometimes are desperate for, an adult advocate, cheerleader, or trusted 'go-to' person who believes in them and stands with them through it all. With certainty, students' actions create reactions—consequences—but, they need genuine guidance in understanding that they own their decisions made in the classroom, cafeteria, hallways, and life which result in either good or bad consequences. Working together to create learning opportunities establishes the atmosphere that students realize that they are worthy, accepted, and understood no matter what! Understanding the reasons our students are the way they are, act, choose, live, or approach situations requires careful listening with our entire minds, hearts, and souls. We may be the only person that our students ever have in their young lives who are there for and with them, helping them find their own place or niche in which they will invest themselves and triumph in success."

*Dr. Mike—Founder and CO-CEO of Forest of The Rain Productions an Education Affairs Organization:*

"In every opportunity to engage a difficult learner, use compassion as a tool to break down barriers to gaining trust and respect. My most effective model is one I call FFC. I let all students know, especially those with a more challenging path to academic success that I am Firm, Fair, and Consistent. The FFC model affords the student a level of comfort they are going to be treated respectfully. Once a student knows the expectation, many successfully navigate their learning experiences."

*Jennifer Bennevento—American Federation of Teachers Professional Development Director:*

"Sometimes, what these difficult students really need is someone to connect to. By taking the time to get to know them and actively working to build that relationship, we as educators show them that they're important.

We demonstrate how much we value them by putting in the effort to build that positive relationship. Showing a student that we genuinely care is the first step toward building trust and respect."

*Dr. Dorothy C. Handfield—Long term educator:*

"When working with challenging youth, consistency is key. You have to be consistent with your expectations. You must be clear with what you will and will not tolerate from the youth. And, your expectations must be clearly explained, so everyone understands. Remember that the youth are listening to your words and watching your actions. So as adults, we have to model the type of behavior that we want from the youth."

# Resources

**Some Resources Mentioned in This Book**

CANDI

CLASS CREED

POST CARDS

THE BLESSING

FLIP FLIPPEN

RUBY PAYNE

MY WEBSITE: www.DanBlanchard.net

MY BLOG: http://granddaddyssecrets.com/blog/

MY NEWSLETTER: http://granddaddyssecrets.com/newsletter-2/

MY BOOK OTHER BOOKS: http://granddaddyssecrets.com/the-books/

# BOOKS BY DANIEL BLANCHARD

### Granddaddy's Secrets

teen leadership book series is sure to capture your imagination on what's really possible with a little help and encouragement, as well as sustained effort and motivation.

*Feeling Lucky?*  *Feeling Good*  *The Storm*  *A Sprint to the Top*

### Professional Education Books

*Success and Social Skills Secrets for Kids*
How 30 days and 150 words can help improve student performance and social emotional learning

*Evaluation of Professional Development in an Urban High School*
Includes Specific Steps to Make PD Successful

### Contributed Author

*A Teachers' Guide to the Common Core*  *Teaching in the Middle and Secondary Schools!*  *Priceless Personalities Success Stories*  *The Expert's Guide to Teenagers*

Website: www.GranddaddysSecrets.com
Amazon Author Page: www.amazon.com/-/e/B00KEO611E
Twitter: @Dan007blanchard
Facebook: facebook.com/daniel.blanchard.186?fref=ts
LinkedIn: linkedin.com/in/daniel-blanchard-82a69723

# ABOUT THE AUTHOR

Dan Blanchard the Award-Winning Author, Speaker, Educator, two-time Junior Olympian Wrestler, and two-time Junior Olympian Wrestling Coach grew up as a student-athlete. However, Dan admits that as a youth he was more of an athlete than a student. Dan has now successfully completed fourteen years of college and has earned seven degrees. He teaches Special Education in Connecticut's largest inner-city high school where he was chosen by the AFT-CT as the face and voice of educational reform and is now on the speaking circuit for them. Dan was with the team that put forth Connecticut's new Social Studies Frameworks and is also a member of the Special Education Advisory Board to the Connecticut State Department of Education. In addition, Dan is a Teacher Consultant for the University of Connecticut's Writing Project. Finally, Dan is a double veteran of the Army and the Air Force.

Because Dan's students repeatedly asked him to write a book to tell others what he tells them, Dan finally listened and has now authored, The Storm: How Young Men Become Good Men. Dan is currently writing The Storm's sequel The Rising Tide. He has also written academic books called, Evaluating Professional Development in An Urban High School and co-authored another book with the American Federation of Teachers called, A Teacher's Guide to the Common Core. Dan has also written, Granddaddy's Success and Social Skills Secrets for Kids: How 30 Days and 150 Words Can Improve Student Performance and Social Emotional Learning. Finally, Dan writes a dozen columns on things from leadership, teens, education, special education, and parenting.

As an educator, coach, tutor, author, speaker, life coach, columnist, blogger and parent, Dan feels that it is his duty to positively influence our youth every chance that he gets! He lives with his wife, Jennifer, their five children, and the family dog in Connecticut.

You can find out more about Dan at www.DanBlanchard.net

Made in the USA
Middletown, DE
22 April 2019